# Choose Ye This Day

# Choose Ye This Day

## How to Effectively Proclaim the Gospel Message

**World Wide Publications**
A ministry of the Billy Graham Evangelistic Association
1303 Hennepin Ave., Minneapolis, Minnesota  55403

**Choose Ye This Day**

World Wide Publications is the publishing ministry of the Billy Graham Evangelistic Association.

Library of Congress Catalog Card Number: 89-050950

ISBN: 0-89066-143-X

Printed in the United States of America

# Contents

# Preface

Human life is filled with decisions. We must make choices every day of our lives—some of them insignificant decisions, some with life-changing consequences. We may resist decision-making, but nevertheless we must choose.

The Bible, too, brings us face-to-face with the necessity of decision. Moses, nearing the end of his life and preparing to turn the leadership of Israel over to Joshua, brought these words from God to his people:

> I have set before you life and death, blessings and curses. Now choose life, so that you and your children may live and that you may love the Lord your God, listen to his voice, and hold fast to him. For the Lord is your life (Deuteronomy 30:19–20).

After Moses' death, Joshua took up the theme of "choosing." He set before the people of God an all-important choice: "Choose for yourselves this day whom you will serve. . . . But as for me and my household, we will serve the Lord" (Joshua 24:15).

The challenge Joshua brought before the children of Israel some 3500 years ago is the same choice faced by men and women today. People still must "choose whom they will serve." They must consciously "choose life," or they have unconsciously chosen death.

For this reason, Christians reach out to those who have not yet chosen in favor of the truth. Whether in large crusades or in individual sharing over a cup of coffee, those of us who know Christ and are devoted to him are called, like Joshua, to turn to those around us and say, "Choose this day whom you will serve."

In a more defined way, pastors and evangelists have the responsibility for presenting the gospel to those who do not know Christ. Men and women in such ministries can look to the example of evangelists such as Billy Graham, Luis Palau, and Leighton Ford, and learn from them the principles of effective evangelism.

*Choose Ye This Day* is a book about decisions—specifically, helping people come to the place of making a choice to follow Jesus Christ and submit to his Lordship. The individuals represented in these chapters are some of the most respected pastors, evangelists, and church leaders of our day; their cumulative experience gives insight and practical help in ministering the gospel of Christ effectively.

# Chapter One
# The Evangelist and a Torn World

*Billy Graham*

We live in the most revolutionary period of world history. In the distance, I can hear the sound of hoofbeats. The four horsemen of the Apocalypse of Revelation are even now riding this way. A mighty, terrible judgment is approaching. Man's sinfulness has the world on a self-destructive course.

You and I, God's ambassadors, are called to sound the warning, to make judgment clear, to call sinners to repentance, to announce God's grace, to point to the Cross and the God-man on the cross, to point to the empty tomb, to shout the Good News from the housetops, to point the way to peace with God and peace between nations.

A French newspaper editorial said recently, "The possibility of an Armageddon before the end of this decade frightens us all." To be God's evangelist in today's torn world is both a thrilling and a fearful thing.

From New York to Moscow, from Caracas to Johannesburg, from Nairobi to Hong Kong, our cities are spiritually and morally dying. And we are called to stand up in our dying cities and villages and proclaim new life in Christ.

The evangelistic harvest is always urgent, but there seem to be periods of special urgency in history when it can be said with peculiar relevance, the fields "are *ripe* for harvest" (John 4:35, emphasis added). I believe that we are now in such a period. Because of technology, this generation is the most critical in modern history, not just for world events but for the advancement of the kingdom of God. And that should give us a sense of urgency greater than anything the church has ever experienced.

Millions of people are searching for answers to the crushing problems and fears they face every day. There is an openness to the gospel in this generation which we may never see again. Almost every newspaper and every book screams from its pages: "The harvest is ripe."

Never have we had more efficient instruments in our hands to help us gather the harvest. Yet at a time when the harvest is the ripest in history, the church often flounders in confusion, especially concerning evangelism.

## The Work of the Evangelist

By definition, an evangelist is a person with a special gift from the Holy Spirit to announce the Good News of the gospel.

The same Greek word that is translated "gospel," "preaching," and other evangelistic words in the New Testament is used over sixty times in Paul's writings alone. Its verb form, meaning "to announce the Good News," occurs over fifty times. The Greek word for *evangelist* means "one who announces the Good News." The word *evangelist* was apparently rare in the ancient world, but is used three times in the New Testament. It is listed as one of the gifts God has given to the church in Ephesians 4:11, "He . . . gave some to be apostles, some to be prophets, some to be evangelists, and some to be pastors and teachers." Philip is termed an evangelist (Acts 21:8), and Timothy is charged by Paul to "do the work of an evangelist" (2 Timothy 4:5).

Two biblical examples—Philip and Timothy—illustrate the work of an evangelist. Philip "preached the good news of the kingdom of God and the name of Jesus Christ" (Acts 8:12). Paul called Timothy "our brother and God's fellow worker in spreading the gospel of Christ" (1 Thessalonians 3:3). An evangelist, then, is one who proclaims the gospel to those who have not accepted it, with the goal of spreading the Good News to them.

The term *evangelism* encompasses every effort to declare the Good News of Jesus Christ, to the end that people may understand God's offer of salvation and respond in faith and discipleship. In the definition of the Lausanne Covenant,

> To evangelize is to spread the good news that Jesus Christ died for our sins and was raised from the dead according to the Scriptures, and that as the reigning Lord he now offers the forgiveness of sins and the liberating gift of the Spirit to all who repent and believe. . . . Evangelism itself is the proclamation of the historical, biblical Christ as Savior and Lord, with a view to persuading people to come to him personally and so be reconciled to God. In issuing the Gospel invitation we have no liberty to conceal the cost of discipleship. . . . The results of evangelism include obedience to Christ, incorporation into his church and responsible service in the world.

At one of the recent Roman Catholic conclaves to choose a new pope, confusing signals were sent out. By custom, the secret ballots of the cardinals are burned after each vote, and black smoke comes billowing out. When a new pope has been elected, a chemical is added so that white smoke comes out to indicate that the decision has been made. At one election, not enough chemical was added and the smoke came out gray. The wondering crowds outside were left in confusion as to whether or not they had a new pope.

A similar confusion exists concerning the work of the evangelist today. And yet we cannot risk confusion if we are to make the impact on our generation that God expects of us. "If the trumpet does not sound a clear call, who will get ready for battle?" (1 Corinthians 14:8).

Today we have scores of definitions of what evangelism is, and what an evangelist is. Some think of evangelism simply in terms of getting more people to join the church. Others define evangelism as attempting to change the structures of society. Some have moved from a belief in man's personal moral responsibility before God, to a concept which declares all men are saved. They say man is not lost; there is no Judgment Day; there is no hell. This spreading "universalism" deadens the urgency of the gospel in some quarters.

But salvation through Christ is a family relationship, not membership in an organization. Evangelism in its biblical sense is concerned with individuals and their relationship to God, and also their relationship and responsibility to others.

During the past three or four years a new emphasis has developed in my own preaching—an emphasis on discipleship. In recent crusades in Florida and Washington State, I stressed the *cost* of following Christ, and yet in two weeks more than fourteen thousand people responded to receive Christ. In addition, thousands who watched our telecasts on television throughout the United States and Canada phoned in for personal counseling each night.

I believe that people, especially young people, respond to a hard challenge. And certainly there has never been a challenge "harder" than that of the Lord Jesus Christ. He never offers cheap grace. He never lowers his standard for entrance to the kingdom of God.

## The Motive of Evangelism

What is our motive in evangelism? What is the motive behind our evangelism? Why did the apostle Paul go from place to place, suffering as few have suffered? Concerning his various sufferings, Paul said in 2 Corinthians 11:25–30 that there was a goal and a purpose in his proclamation that made him even boast in his weakness. The apostle Paul had a life-changing encounter with Christ on the Damascus road, and he told it over and over.

The first motive is found in Paul's words in 2 Corinthians 5:14: "Christ's love compels us." I am convinced the greatest act of love we can ever perform for others is to tell them about God's love for them in Christ.

Often we are asked about the relationship between social

action and evangelism. While evangelism has priority, social action and social concern go hand in hand. We must take a strong stand for racial understanding. We must have a burden that goes beyond just "concern." We must do something about world hunger. We must work and pray for world peace when the nations are arming themselves to the teeth, getting ready for what will be Armageddon.

A bishop of the Church of England once told me that he did not know of one great social movement in his country that did not have its roots in some evangelical awakening, quite often because of evangelistic preaching. Some of the greatest social movements in history have been the fruit of true evangelical revival led by the preaching of God-anointed evangelists.

Where missionaries went around the world carrying the message of Christ's redeeming love, hospitals, schools, orphanages, and leprosariums were built, and hundreds of other good works followed. Many missiologists will admit the mistakes some missionaries made in various parts of the world, yet it is quite easy to criticize them in hindsight! Hundreds of them were separated from loved ones for years on end. Hundreds suffered martyrdom in order to bring the light of the gospel to various parts of the world. Those early missionaries brought the message of the gospel to the United States.

Another motive for evangelism is the approaching Judgment. Paul said, "Since, then, we know what it is to fear the Lord, we try to persuade men" (2 Corinthians 5:11). When Paul preached his great sermon at Mars Hill in Athens, he said, "God . . . commands all people everywhere to repent. For he has set a day when he will judge the world with justice by the man he has appointed" (Acts 17:30–31).

A Judgment Day is approaching. Even the secular world is talking more and more about Armageddon and the end of the world. A newspaper columnist in England wrote recently, "Sometimes I get the feeling I am sitting on a hilltop watching two trains race toward each other on the same track."

This is a time for the Christian evangelist to proclaim the hope of the return of Jesus Christ, coupled with a warning of impending judgment. In the solemn light of that Day of

Judgment, humanity's greatest need is for reconciliation with God.

But our primary motive, in my view, is the command of our Commander-in-chief, the Lord Jesus Christ. We engage in evangelism today not because we want to, or because we choose to, or because we like to, but because *we have been told to*. We are under orders. Our Lord has commanded us to go, to preach, to make disciples—and that should be enough for us. Evangelistic inactivity is disobedience. The so-called Great Commission occurs five times in the Bible—at the end of each of the four Gospels, and once at the beginning of Acts. I am sure that he repeated these commands many times.

If there were no visible results, the command would still be enough. It is not optional. We have no choice. We are ambassadors under authority.

## The Message of Evangelism

In recent years, many have rejected the biblical doctrine that men are individually sinners before God and will be held responsible to him at the Judgment. Instead, they believe in a doctrine of collective sinfulness and of the corporate guilt of society. I accept the fact that sin affects society as a whole, and we must take that seriously. But we are in danger of neglecting the need for personal repentance of sin and faith in the Lord Jesus Christ. We are forgetting the emphatic "must" in "You *must* be born again."

Peter proclaimed, "Salvation is found in no one else, for there is no other name under heaven given to men by which we must be saved" (Acts 4:12).

The great Methodist preacher of London, Dr. Leslie Weatherhead, once wrote that there are many things we don't know about hell, but that Jesus used every image in his power to tell us that hell is real, that it is terrible, that it is something to be feared, that it is something to avoid. The most compassionate person who ever lived, Jesus, spoke of outer darkness, a closed door, gnashing of teeth, and the lake of fire.

Three years ago I listened to one of the greatest challenges to me that I have ever had, from an unexpected source. We were just beginning our crusade in Osaka, Japan. At a wonderful reception for us with hundreds of leaders of Osaka and Kyoto, the governor of Osaka, in his brief address of welcome, turned to me and asked, "Dr. Graham, why is it that the church in Japan is about the same as it was in the seventeenth century?" He said, "I believe it is because the gospel has not been made clear to the Japanese people. I hope that you will make it clear."

There are millions in America and Europe for whom the gospel has not been made clear. We have failed in our communication, so that people have only a hazy idea of what it means to be a true follower of Jesus Christ.

At the time of the 1960 Olympics, a magazine cartoon parodied the classic story of the runner from Marathon. The runner, carrying the message of victory, came stumbling and gasping into the palace, fell prostrate before the king, and with a puzzled, blank look on his face, mumbled, "I have forgotten the message." There are times when I hear preaching on the radio and even on television, or read religious periodicals—and I sometimes wonder if we have forgotten the message.

Jesus Christ by his death and resurrection *became* the gospel. It is not just a new set of morals, or a guide for happy living. It is the solemn message that we are alienated from God, and only Christ by his death and resurrection can save us.

In the New Testament we are promised suffering, persecution, and death as followers of the Lord Jesus Christ. Any message other than the gospel of Jesus Christ is not evangelism. Paul sums up this gospel in 1 Corinthians 15:3–4: "Christ died for our sins according to the Scriptures, . . . he was buried, . . . he was raised on the third day according to the Scriptures."

## The Methods of Evangelism

If we go back two thousand years in history to the origin of our Great Commission, we find various methods of preaching Christ. Pentecost, that great outpouring of the Holy Spirit on the early church, was followed shortly by persecution. Under persecution, the little church was scattered, very much as a farmer scatters seed. Wherever they went, they used whatever method was available: the synagogue, until they were cast out of it; the street corners, until they were thrown into prison. Then they used the prisons themselves. Later, they wrote letters. We have some of the letters of the disciples like Peter, Paul, Luke, and John. They wrote books. Later on, gospel tracts were written. And after a while came more books, like those of Augustine of Hippo. Christians used every available means to proclaim the gospel of Christ.

We, too, need to explore every legitimate method for reaching our world for Christ. New challenges call for new methods and new strategies.

But important as they may be, methods and organization alone are not enough. We are involved in a spiritual battle. The evangelist and the work of evangelism are opposed on every hand by Satan and his forces. When the seed of the gospel is being sown, the Enemy is always there sowing the tares and blinding the minds of those whom we seek to evangelize. Let us not underestimate the strategy of Satan. He uses every kind of deception, force, and error to try to destroy the effectiveness of the gospel. But we know that "greater is he that is in us than he that is in the world." We need to trust the Holy Spirit to guide, lead, and direct us, just as we trust the Holy Spirit for the results in our evangelism, because he alone can give success. That is why prayer is such a critical part of evangelism.

Whatever human methods we employ, God's method for evangelism is men and women. God uses men and women who have been filled and anointed and called by the Holy Spirit, and are in turn witnessing for him wherever God sends them. We are now living in a generation when nothing will break through the overwhelming power of Satan except the supernatural power of the Holy Spirit.

Fifteen centuries ago Augustine, Bishop of Hippo (modern Tunisia), heard the terrible news that a great city was dying. Rome—capital of the known world, cultural center, business hub—was in flames. Pagan armies were overwhelming Rome, and Augustine felt the pain of that dying city.

Later, in his great work, *The City of God*, Augustine wrote, "The city that man is building will always die. . . . The city that God builds will never die."

Our newspapers tell of the cities people build and of their destruction by human sinfulness. The Bible, God's holy Word, tells of the city that God is building for mankind's salvation. The evangelist is called to stand in the ruins of "the city of man" and proclaim the truth of the city that God is building.

John Wesley told his coworkers, "You have nothing to do but save souls. Therefore spend and be spent in this work. . . . It is not your business to preach so many times, and to take care of this or that society; but to save as many souls as you can; to bring as many sinners as you possibly can to repentance, and with all your power to build them up in that holiness without which they cannot see the Lord."

D. L. Moody used to go into the streets of Chicago, giving out tracts and talking to everyone he met about Jesus Christ. He was called "crazy Moody."

William Booth, founder of the Salvation Army, was a wild young lad of seventeen in the town of Nottingham, England. He heard that an American evangelist had come to town. He was eager to hear this stranger from the New World, with his funny accent and his great stories. But when he went, he was transfixed by the message of the gospel. He saw the unholiness and sinfulness of his heart and the demands of God before him.

He said that he was almost transported into another world. When the invitation to receive Christ was given, this young boy responded, and out of that conversion came the worldwide ministry of the Salvation Army, feeding people who are physically hungry, offering salvation to the spiritually hungry.

An American man, a humble preacher of the gospel, went back to that chapel in England where Booth was converted. And when he thought of the souls that had been won and the people who had been blessed by Christ through the ministry of William Booth, he placed his hand on the bronze marker that identified the place of Booth's conversion, and prayed aloud, "Do it again, Lord. Lord, do it again."

Lord, do it again. Do what you did when the apostles were called. Do what you did following Pentecost. Do whatever needs to be done in each of our hearts. Lord, enlarge our vision. Do it again.

*This chapter is taken from Dr. Graham's message, "The Evangelist and a Torn World," delivered at the 1983 International Conference for Itinerant Evangelists in Amsterdam.*

# Chapter Two
# The Evangelist's Heart

## *Luis Palau*

"Why him?" More than a few people asked that question during D. L. Moody's evangelistic campaigns throughout Great Britain during the 1870s. Multiplied thousands were coming to faith in Jesus Christ, and whole cities were beginning to sing the praises of God. The impact of the gospel was astonishing.

Yet Moody himself was anything but extraordinary. His education was limited. His speech was unimpressive. His messages were short and simple. Nevertheless, everywhere Moody preached hundreds came forward publicly to confess the Lord Jesus as Savior.

In Birmingham, England, one theologian went so far as to tell Moody: "The work is most plainly from God, for I can see no relation between yourself and what you have done."

Moody laughed and replied, "I should be very sorry if it were otherwise."

Thousands of evangelists have proclaimed the gospel throughout the world during the closing centuries of this millennium. But we look back and say that only a few, such as Moody, were truly great. Why do we call them great and how can we be like them?

The answer has little to do with method or technique. Some

preached before the masses, some in churches. Some presented the gospel in small groups, some one-on-one. Most of the great evangelists used a combination of approaches. But that isn't what made them great.

The great evangelists of the past all shared ten characteristics which gave them a tremendous heart for the world. Both Scripture and church history speak to the importance of these characteristics which should shape every Christian's heart and life.

## 1. Passion

Booth, Calvin, Finney, Luther, Moody, Spurgeon, Sunday, Sung, ten Boom, Wesley, Whitefield, Zinzendorf, Zwingli, and all the other truly great evangelists of the past had a passion for souls which burned within them.

"I remind you," Paul said in 2 Timothy 1:6–7, "to fan into flame the gift of God, which is in you through the laying on of my hands." Why? "For God did not give us a spirit of timidity, but a spirit of power, of love and of self-discipline." The first characteristic that ought to mark the evangelist is the fire of the Holy Spirit.

I happened to meet Corrie ten Boom at the 1974 Lausanne Congress on World Evangelization. She couldn't get up, so I knelt down beside her couch and heard Corrie say, "I love my Jesus," with that distinctive, unforgettable Dutch accent of hers. "I love my Jesus." That love compelled her to proclaim Jesus Christ in more than sixty nations and lead many thousands to faith in Jesus Christ. What fire for her Jesus that woman had, what a passion for souls!

But it's possible for us to look at someone we consider great and then simply copy their mannerisms and phraseology. The temptation to work up imitation fire instead of experiencing the Holy Spirit's work in our own hearts can be enormous, especially for those of us trying to reach the masses. There is a desire to be seen. We want to draw attention. But there is a great difference between drawing attention to our Savior and calling attention to ourselves.

The men and women whom we call great obviously caught the imagination and attention of the multitudes, but we remember them most because of the impact they made in people's lives. The fire of the Holy Spirit burned within them.

## 2. Gospel

When we read the sermons of the great evangelists of the past, we discover that they were incredibly Christ-centered. If we look at their messages word for word, it is wonderful gospel.

Evangelists are called by God to promote Jesus Christ. We are his public relations people. We are his proclaimers. We are his ambassadors. We come to town to talk about Jesus, not to be taken up by sideshows or enthralled by our gifts.

How can I be an evangelist if my theme is not Jesus Christ? Some other message may be wonderful. It may be intriguing. It may even be of God. But an evangelist preaches Jesus Christ. Some people think that helping the poor is the gospel, but such ministry is a result of the gospel. Others emphasize the gifts for healing the sick. Healing may be a tremendous sign of God's power, but it isn't the gospel itself.

Whatever gifts the Spirit gives us, we need to practice. But when we are serving as evangelists, we either preach Jesus Christ or we're not preaching the gospel. We may have exciting programs with great music, hand clapping, arm waving, and people coming forward. But are we preaching the gospel?

Paul summarizes the Good News that we preach in this way:

> I want to remind you of the gospel I preached to you, which you received and on which you have taken your stand. By this gospel you are saved, if you hold firmly to the word I preached to you. Otherwise, you have believed in vain.
>
> For what I received I passed on to you as of first importance: that Christ died for our sins according to the Scriptures, that he was buried, that he was raised on the third day according to the Scrip-

tures, and that he appeared to Peter, and then to the Twelve. After that, he appeared to more than five hundred of the brothers at the same time (1 Corinthians 15:1–6).

The message of the gospel is that Jesus Christ died for our sins, was buried, and was raised on the third day. If we do not agree from the heart that this message is of "first importance," we have no gospel message to present to the world.

## 3. Holiness

The great evangelists were holy men and women of God. Holiness isn't a movement; it's a life walked in the light, being transparent before God and others. Of all the servants of God in the world, evangelists are the most scrutinized, and rightly so. If we've tried to hide any sin, we need to confess it and clear it up immediately. After all, our greatest joy is to walk in the light. "If you think sin is fun," the Rev. John MacArthur says, "you should try holiness." It's much more exciting.

We must not confuse holiness with the gifts of the Spirit. Some people say, "I must be filled with the Spirit, because I have this (or that) gift." We can argue with the Lord and say, "But Lord, thirty-five people came forward last night. Did you hear about the drunkard who was converted?" We can sell ourselves on the idea that we are filled with the Spirit because so many are coming to faith in Jesus Christ. But people come to Christ because we preach the gospel, and God always honors the gospel. The state of our own souls is a far different issue.

Billy Graham once pointed out that most evangelists don't last more than ten years. The temptation to give up is sometimes overwhelming. But evangelists even more frequently dishonor the name of the Lord because of lack of holiness in the areas of money, sex, and pride. I've personally known several powerful evangelists who today are on the sidelines. They're finished, because they did not walk in holiness. They confused the gift with the walk.

## 4. Vision

Wesley, Moody, Booth, and others were people with vision. We need to have a big vision, too. The Lord will not necessarily make us into national or international evangelists, as the journalists might call us, but a large vision gives us perspective and stability.

Vision is like going through a storm in an airplane. In a single engine airplane, we get tossed up and down and side to side by every bit of turbulence. Flying in a jumbo jet is a different story; they don't get tossed around much in a storm. Those big wings give stability. When we have a big vision, the wings move a little, but the airplane doesn't rock very much. If our vision is small, however, the little airplane may feel like it's falling apart. Vision helps us to go through the clouds and the storms without being shaken and tempted to give up.

Christ certainly never limited his disciples' vision. Even though he restricted his own public ministry to Palestine, he came and died for all mankind. And after his resurrection, he commissioned his followers to "make disciples of *all* nations" (Matthew 28:19, emphasis added), and sent them to Jerusalem, then to all Judea and Samaria, and ultimately to the ends of the earth.

During the crucial, formative years of the New Testament church, God used the apostle Paul in a tremendous way. Even his opponents admitted that he had saturated entire provinces with the gospel and turned the world upside down. He had a big strategy—big enough to reach the entire Roman Empire, and big enough to give him stability when the going was rough.

During the 1700s Wesley said, "The world is my parish." He faced intense opposition across Britain. But when told to stay in Oxford, Wesley refused to comply. And like Wesley, we must not hide our message and limit our vision when so many have yet to hear the Good News of Jesus Christ in our day.

## 5. Boldness

Those we call great were men and women of holy audacity. Calvin confronted the entire French church. Luther boldly confronted the Holy Roman Empire. Zinzendorf had the boldness to send missionaries and evangelists to the West Indies, and he went as well. Whitefield preached the gospel up and down the British countryside and in America, despite the threat of ridicule and mob violence. These evangelists had holy audacity. Like them, we must learn to launch out, in the name of the Lord, take risks, and even face death with courage.

An evangelist is often looked at as a leader within the body of Christ. Therefore, even under threat, we have to keep going on. "I consider my life worth nothing to me," Paul said, "if only I may finish the race and complete the task the Lord Jesus has given me—the task of testifying to the gospel of God's grace" (Acts 20:24).

On occasion I've been confronted by militant guerrillas who threatened to assassinate me. I've wanted to get on an airplane and say, "Good-bye, Peru, I'll see you in heaven. Somebody else can evangelize you." But I had to stop and think: "I'm a servant of the Lord. The Master was crucified. People are looking for courageous leadership and selfless abandon. I must get on with it in the name of Jesus Christ."

Holy audacity also prompts us to try new approaches. Some of us may be led to use an approach that older folks will question. But we should try it anyway in the name of the Lord, with humility, under counsel. We don't have to do everything the way it has always been done. As far as I'm concerned, any method is valid as long as it is ethical and moral. There are no biblical restraints on methodology, only on the message. The message is sacred and it never changes. The methods need to vary, depending on whom we're trying to reach with the gospel.

The biographies of the great evangelists reveal that they took hold of any method in order to saturate the cities and the masses with the gospel. In God's name they even sanctified the media to communicate the gospel of Jesus Christ.

Somebody once asked me, "Do you think if Jesus were here, he would be on television?" Of course. If Paul were here, would he have a press conference? Definitely. He would do anything to get the attention of the city.

Those we call great were highly recognized because they took advantage of unique "new" methods, sanctified them, and used them to evangelize the masses. I believe God also would have us dream about how to use various media to get the attention of people and point them to Jesus Christ.

## 6. Criticism

From least to greatest, all true evangelists have been criticized, attacked, and even persecuted. That shouldn't surprise us, for "everyone who wants to live a godly life in Christ Jesus will be persecuted" (2 Timothy 3:12).

Some people think, "If I'm walking with God, everybody will applaud me and think highly of me." But most people who evangelize create waves. And when we create waves, a lot of people get upset.

Scripture says, "Woe to you when all men speak well of you" (Luke 6:26). It's nice to be well spoken of; I definitely prefer that to criticism. Nevertheless, it's a sign that you're doing something right when certain people begin to get upset because of what you represent and preach.

Calvin saw himself as "only a humble evangelist of our Lord Jesus Christ." But he knew what it was to face severe criticism and attacks. Luther faced intense persecution, too, but when we read the words of his hymn, "A Mighty Fortress Is Our God," we don't pick up a sense of defeat. Instead, Luther seems to be declaring, "I'm going to beat the Devil," even though he was running from those who were trying to kill him. And we honor him today.

Spurgeon founded a large church in London, but was really more of an evangelist than a pastor. He too was ridiculed, put down, and insulted. Most evangelists are. Even Billy Graham has faced times when people have insulted and cut him down.

Yet he has redeemed the term "evangelist" from the 1920s and 1930s, when to be called an evangelist was an insult in many countries. Like him, we are called to be godly men and women who exemplify integrity and righteousness in this generation.

## 7. Church

When we analyze the great evangelists of the past, we'll find that they saw themselves as active members of the body of Christ and servants of the church.

Ephesians 4:11–12 says that God "gave some to be apostles, some to be prophets, some to be evangelists, and some to be pastors and teachers." Why? "To prepare God's people for works of service, so that the body of Christ may be built up."

Our job is to lift up Jesus Christ and build up his church. We point to sin, but only to show that the Cross liberates us, and that the Resurrection revolutionizes us. We are not to begin pointing out the flaws and weaknesses of the church in front of the world.

A few evangelists erred on this point during part of the course of their ministry. Whitefield, for instance, made the mistake of publicly attacking the clergy. We all run that risk if we confuse our calling. Evangelists are not prophets. One who is called to be a prophet to the church, is not an evangelist. We must learn to differentiate between the two.

Evangelists who have a burden for the church will come in to revive it by the power of the Holy Spirit. If they have any criticism to make, they should offer it to the leadership in private, behind closed doors.

If I were a pastor, I wouldn't invite an evangelist to my city unless I first found out what church he and his family belonged to, and then talked with that church's elders or deacons to find out how active he is within that fellowship. Does he attend when he is home just like everyone else, or does he feel superior because he travels so much? Is he subject to church discipline, or is he exempt because he is better known than others?

We should see ourselves as nothing but slaves of Jesus

Christ and servants of his church. Our goal should be to work "with the church, through the church, and for the church" as we seek to obey Christ's Great Commission.

## 8. Love

God's greatest servants in the past learned to love the body of Jesus Christ after they saw their own weaknesses. As the years went by, they realized how much they were growing and learning. Secondary denominational issues weren't as important as they once thought. They began to understand that the body of Christ includes everyone who belongs to Jesus Christ.

These great servants didn't compromise the basic truth of the gospel. But many of us attended rather closed fellowships when we were younger. The feeling was, "We're the only good Christians in town. We know the truth. Everyone else is off track. Why even bother to pray for them?"

But as we grow in the Lord, we begin to realize that people who love Jesus Christ are beautiful people. We may not see eye-to-eye with others on everything. But if we truly know and love Christ, we're all part of the same body.

What we're talking about is quite different from merely structural ecumenism, which overlooks the truth for the sake of a unity lacking in foundational solidity. "You don't believe Jesus was born of the Virgin Mary? Oh, that's all right. We're one big happy family." Now there's a difference between *that* sort of ecumenism and the true unity of the body of Christ, of those who accept the basic truths of Christianity.

What are the basic truths? The Apostles' Creed tells us. Anyone who believes that from a pure heart is a brother or sister in Christ. Of course, there is much more to believe, too. Some of us get worked up about one point of doctrine, and some about another. But those we call the great evangelists of the past learned that we can afford to have differences on secondary issues.

Secondary issues are important. We don't pretend that they don't matter to us anymore. We have our convictions. We have our distinctives. We don't give them up, but we say to each other, "I love you in Jesus Christ. I can see the presence of God in your life. Together, let's evangelize for the sake of the lost."

## 9. Prayer

When we read about the great evangelists of the past, we discover that each one learned the secret of prayer in his or her own way. Luther used to get up at four o'clock each morning. "Just as the business of the tailor is to make clothing, and that of the shoemaker to mend shoes," he said, "so the business of the Christian is to pray." The secret of Luther's revolutionary life was his commitment to spend time alone with God every day.

Finney had a prayer partner called Father Nash who traveled with him. Father Nash didn't preach. Most people never knew he was in town. He often would stay out in the woods praying morning, noon, and night for Finney, for each meeting, and for the outpouring of the Holy Spirit of God.

Moody began each of his evangelistic campaigns by urging all of God's people to pray. He once said, "We ought to see the face of God every morning before we see the face of man. If you have so much business to attend to that you have no time to pray, depend upon it that you have more business on hand than God ever intended."

## 10. Faithfulness

The nine characteristics enumerated above actually apply to almost any servant of Jesus Christ. But one more characteristic sets the great evangelists of the past apart from the rest: They evangelized aggressively until their dying hour.

Moody left the pulpit one night absolutely worn out, was sent home immediately under medical care, and died some days later. Whitefield told a friend, "I had rather wear out than rust out." On another occasion he remarked, "I intend going on till I drop." Like Moody, he died in the middle of an evangelistic campaign.

Another example of faithfulness to the gospel in our own day is Billy Graham. We were invited to Glasgow, Scotland, for an evangelistic campaign about twenty-five years after Dr. Graham had a crusade there. There the story was told of an old Church of Scotland minister who had gone to hear Billy Graham each evening. When the crusade was over the minister said, "Dr. Graham, I've heard you every night for six weeks, and you've preached the same sermon every single night." Except for the introduction and illustrations, that's been true throughout Dr. Graham's worldwide gospel ministry.

An evangelist preaches the same message over and over. There's no variation. Our introductory themes change each time, but eventually about halfway through each message, we speak about the Cross, the Resurrection, repentance, faith, and commitment. Otherwise, we haven't preached the gospel.

Our sermon titles, introductions, and illustrations add color. Other than that, every message is the same. Some Christians may come and say, "Oh, phooey, I've heard this all before." Of course they've heard it before! We're not preaching for them. We're trying to reach the lost.

When we look at the world around us, what do we see? What is God saying to our hearts? Do we feel his compassion for those without hope and without God in the world?

I believe God desires to cultivate within us a heart that loves the world like he does—enough to keep relentlessly caring whether others hear the gospel, believe in Jesus Christ, and become his disciples. We need to take the Great Commission seriously.

Scripture tells us that when Jesus saw the lost multitudes, "He had compassion on them, because they were harassed and helpless, like sheep without a shepherd" (Matthew 9:36). We need to ask God to move our hearts with the same compassion that moves his heart.

*Luis Palau, an evangelist with an international ministry, is founder and president of the Luis Palau Evangelistic Association. This chapter was originally published as a booklet titled,* Heart for the World *(OMF Literature, Inc., for the 1989 Second International Congress on World Evangelization, in Manila).*

# Chapter Three
# A View
# From the Pew

*Tom Houston*

The parable of the sower and the seed (Matthew 13:1–23) is a two-edged sword. With one side it cuts through the discouragement we are tempted to feel when people do not respond or when they fall away. It is reassuring that even Jesus found it so. The other edge, however, slays us for the laziness and carelessness with which we sometimes approach our task.

The task of communication is not an easy one. Often our attempts at communication are distorted by misunderstanding: we speak out of one set of assumptions, and our hearers listen through their own grid of past experience, personal prejudice, and misinformation.

This parable, like many of the stories Jesus told, gives us a profound insight into the nature of communicating the gospel. As we grasp these truths, understanding the process of communication and comprehension in our audience, we can be better equipped to share the gospel effectively.

## It's Not What We Say, It's What They Hear

Jesus concluded, "'Listen then, if you have ears" (Matthew

13:9, TEV). There is as much emphasis in the Bible on hearing as on speaking. Evangelists have a great urge, even a need, to speak; but when our need to speak is more important to us than the audience's need to hear, we are in trouble. A lay member of a Baptist church in Russia was pleading for opportunities to preach. But he was not a gifted preacher. He said to his pastor, "Woe is me if I preach not the gospel." The leader struggled to keep from saying, "And woe is the people, if you do!" The audience is of primary importance.

Whenever communication is attempted, three elements are present:

Speaker/Source     Message     Hearer/Receptor

In this case (Matthew 13:10) these are:

Jesus        Parables        The People

His disciples asked Jesus, "Why do *you* use *parables* when you talk to *the people?*" He answered, "The knowledge about the secrets of the Kingdom of heaven has been given to *you*, but not to *them*" (vv. 10–11, TEV, emphasis added). The disciples were learning that Jesus took different approaches to different audiences. His preaching was not an instrument with only one string.

And this was so in spite of the fact that he recognized unconditionally God's part in the process. "The knowledge . . . has been *given* to you, but not to them" (v. 11, emphasis added). We cannot ignore what Jesus said about different approaches to different audiences just because of the place that the authority and power of the Holy Spirit has in the process.

Indeed, Jesus drew on the Bible itself to help him understand his audience. He said, "The prophecy of Isaiah applies to them" (v. 14), and proceeded to apply to the people he had just been addressing from the boat what the prophet said when he was called to his ministry (Isaiah 6). We need to understand what the Bible says about how people react to the Word of God. It's not what we *say* but what they *hear* that matters.

# It's Not How We End but Where We Start

One of the verses that we like least in the Gospels is, "The person who has something will be given more, so that he will have more than enough; but the person who has nothing will have taken away from him even the little he has" (Matthew 13:12, TEV). Jesus applied this truth to the matter of talents and their use (Matthew 25:25; Luke 19:26). He applied it here to knowledge and its acquisition. New knowledge has to be linked to existing knowledge, and if we do not keep adding to our knowledge, we lose it.

This concept has great importance for evangelists. We will achieve nothing unless we get the attention of the audience by building on what they already know. This is why Jesus used parables. To "tell people things that are unknown since the creation of the world," he built on what the people already knew by using parables about familiar things.

To build on existing references, we need to know as much as we can about our audience. How do we do it? What kind of things do we need to know? The range of Jesus' parables and sayings is a good guide. It shows he was quick at "observational audience research," just noticing what made the world go around in peoples' lives.

Jesus kept his eyes open in people's houses, for *home and family* are the greater part of any person's life. He knew a lot about kitchens where the leaven made the dough rise. He saw children ask for the bread when it came out of the grass-fired ovens, and knew that they liked fish and eggs—but not without salt. He observed cleanliness, sometimes obsessive cleanliness, in washing up.

He knew how exciting weddings were, and how heartbreaking funerals were. He saw the differences between children, and hostility between brothers. He knew about the bother of unreliable servants who became drunk or helped themselves to what did not belong to them.

Jesus was familiar with the *work situations* of his hearers. He knew about farms. Plowing, sowing, weeding, and harvesting figure in his parables. Sheep, oxen, hens, and dogs all came into his examples. He knew about vines, figs, and mustard trees. He was familiar with the marketplace with its pearl merchants and traders and fortune hunters. He was at ease with fishermen and builders and soldiers—the whole work scene of his audiences.

He observed *social conditions*—crime, the courts, the prisons, the banquets of the rich, and the misery of the poor. He knew about sickness and doctors and their bills. He sensed impatience with neighbors and antipathy to strangers, and noticed the commonplaces of conversation.

The *world of nature* made its impression on him—the wind in the trees and flowers, and sparrows, eagles, foxes, camels, wolves, serpents, and their ways.

They all appear in his parables and sayings. Why? Because that is what people knew about. And he had to build on that if he were to introduce them to the unknown love and grace of the Father who sent him. This was vital if he was to secure their attention and hold their interest.

Some other features about the parables worked to draw the hearers' interest. They were used in an unpredictable way. The easiest way to lose attention is to be predictable. With Jesus there was always that unexpected turn to the way he took the familiar and used it.

His parables were stories, and everyone stops for a good story. Good storytelling heightens interest.

He left a lot to his hearers. Often they needed to supply the meaning for themselves. That is why the disciples asked what he meant. In this way the people ended up saying things to themselves that they would have resented if he had dared to say them directly. Jesus did not have the urge most preachers have—to say it all, every time.

Listeners are like a radio; they have an "off switch" in their heads. We can preach, and people can totally screen us out. This is what Jesus described as the seed that fell on the hard-trodden path. The truth did not even get a hearing. It was screened out because of the other traffic over that ground.

Knowledge of our audience and the skill to build on what they already know in a way that arouses their curiosity, are essential factors in getting their attention. There are more formal ways of doing this. Opinion polls, books on sociology, psychology, and cultural anthropology can help. We can, however, as Jesus did, get to know people just by keeping our own eyes and ears open.

"The person who has nothing will have taken away from him even the little he has" (v. 12). Some of that tragic result will be the responsibility of the listener. Often, however, evangelists harden their hearers by being entirely predictable, insensitive to their audience, and skilled only in activating the "off button" in their hearers' heads. It's not how you *end* but where you *start* that matters.

## It's Not Just What They Hear, It's What They See

In Jesus' use of the Isaiah passage, he repeated four times the words: seeing, hearing, understanding, eyes, ears, and minds or hearts. Every time he said *see* as well as *hear*. This is not accidental; it has a natural as well as a spiritual significance.

We imagine that what we say is all-important. We are mistaken. People hear our words, but see our body language. How close do we stand to people, or how far away? Sometimes one distance is appropriate, sometimes another is. "The crowd . . . was so large that he got into a boat and sat in it, while the crowd stood on the shore" (Matthew 13:2, TEV). They needed to see Jesus, so he got into a boat. He sat because teachers in those days sat to teach. Sitting communicated authority. When we go up into a high pulpit, six feet above contradiction, it says something. Sometimes this is good. Sometimes it is not.

The Gospels often describe the body language of Jesus. He stretched out his hand and touched a leper (Matthew 8:3). He showed surprise at the Roman officer (Matthew 8:10). He slept through a storm in a boat, then he got up and ordered the winds to cease (Matthew 8:24–26). He touched the eyes of the blind (Matthew 9:29). His heart was filled with pity for leaderless people (Matthew 9:36). He took the five loaves and two fishes, looked up to heaven, and gave thanks to God (Matthew 14:19). He did the same at the Last Supper (Matthew 26:26ff), and it was this body language that led the two on the road to Emmaus to recognize him.

Often it was a look, as with the rich young ruler (Mark 10:21), and it was with Peter when he denied him (Luke 22:61). When they brought to him the woman taken in adultery, they made her stand before them all, but he bent over and wrote on the ground with his finger. Then he straightened up and spoke to them about throwing the first stone. Then he bent over again and wrote on the ground while they all left. And with only the woman still standing there. He straightened up and asked her, "Where are they?" (John 8:3–11). The Lord's body language spoke volumes.

He turned his back on Peter when Peter tried to dissuade him from the cross (Matthew 16:23). He placed his hands on the children (Matthew 19:15). He wept at the grave of Lazarus, and they said, "See how much he loved him." He washed and dried their feet with a towel. The same night he indicated his betrayer sensitively by dipping bread and giving it to Judas. He knelt in the garden, then threw himself on his face. His body language evoked trust. For communication to be successful, the hearer must trust the speaker. The way we stand and sit, our facial expressions, the way we use our hands, our dress, all convey the real, inner person and increase or decrease trust.

If we are part of the community where we preach, people see us not only when we are speaking but at other times. People saw Jesus healing the sick, doing good of every kind, accepting all kinds and classes of people, high and low, rich and poor, educated and less educated. They saw his loyalty to his followers, his attitudes toward his enemies. With some, it created trust. With others, it created fear. He said, "He that has seen me has seen the Father." Because God, the ultimate source of our message, is unseen, it is important that what people see in us creates trust in a believable God. It is not just what they *hear*, it is what they *see* that matters.

## It's Not Just the Message, It's the Meaning

After seeing with the eyes and hearing with the ears must come an understanding of the message in the mind of the listeners. The evangelist can deliver a message, but only the hearers can give it meaning, and that meaning depends on how they can fit the message into all that they already know. They live in their own world with a whole set of beliefs, ideas, and values. These all color what they hear. If the truths being preached do not fit well with the world view of the hearers, several results can occur:

(a) *It can make no sense at all.* A prospective Japanese convert from Shintoism remarked to a painstaking explanation of the Trinity, "Most High Person of Honorable Father, him I understand. Honorable Son, him also I understand. But, please, be so favorable as to tell me, who is that Honorable Bird?" The idea of the dove as a symbol of the Holy Spirit was totally strange.

(b) *It can lead to misunderstanding and rejection.* A crowd of African high school boys once viewed a modern film version of the parable of the rich fool. In the treatment, a greedy, foolish father represented the rich fool. The person who withstood his foolishness and did nothing to prevent his downfall was his son. The point of the parable was lost entirely because the boys just could not see, according to their values, how a son could ever fail to support his father. The gospel could not be pursued further that night. They were entirely distracted.

(c) *It can lead to a distorted version of the gospel.* This is the situation with the seed that fell on shallow ground. The hearers accepted a gospel that they thought promised them a prosperous and easy life. When trouble and persecution arose, this was not what they expected, and they gave up following.

Getting the right meaning in the minds of the listener is always more difficult if the person speaking is from a different culture than his hearers. When Paul preached in Antioch (Acts 13), he used many references to the Old Testament, because his hearers were Jews and knew the Scriptures. When he spoke in Athens, however (Acts 17), he did not quote the Bible at all to his entirely Greek audience. Instead, he quoted their own poets to confirm what he was saying, and let their context give meaning to his message. It is not just the *message*, it is the *meaning* which matters.

## It's Not Just the Truth but the Worth of What We Say

When a message has been understood, a critical point has been reached in the hearer. Jesus used parables to give his audience a chance to fasten on his indirect way of stating the truths of the kingdom and to join the disciples, who did see, hear, and understand. In commenting on how fortunate the disciples were, Jesus gave a clue to successful communication. He referred to people in the past who "wanted very much to see what you see, but they could not, and to hear what you hear, but they did not" (Matthew 13:17, TEV). These prophets and good people set a high value on knowing and serving Messiah. They would have given everything to live when he came, and would have joined his ranks.

The value put on a message determines whether the hearers will retain it or act upon it. That value has to come from the needs that a person wants satisfied.

Everyone wants something. Jesus kept saying to people like blind Bartimaeus, "What do you want me to do for you?" Sometimes he detected it without their saying anything, like the woman of Samaria, or Zacchaeus. Sometimes they said it before he asked, like the rich young ruler, who wanted eternal life. In his case, the young man did not want eternal life enough to let his wealth go, and so he went away unchanged. Zacchaeus and the woman of Samaria saw that Jesus could meet their needs, and they believed in him. Everyone has to come the same way. Unless the new pearl is seen to be worth more than all the old ones, there will be no response. Unless the treasure is worth selling everything for, in order to buy both the field and the treasure, there will be no transaction. Unless people are ready to give up all they have, they will not become disciples of Jesus.

The worth of the gospel to the individual is as impc
its objective truth, and we need to take this into account when
we preach it. We need to speak to what people are hungry for
as we present Jesus. It may not be forgiveness first. It maybe
acceptance first, like Zacchaeus. It may be healing first, like the
man at the pool of Bethesda. It may be a new identity, like
Simon who had the prospect of becoming Peter. It may be a
purpose in life, like James and John who wanted to be fishers of
men. It may be physical safety, like the Philippian jailer. They
all came to need and want forgiveness, but that was not the
need they first felt.

We need to recognize the needs that people themselves feel,
and not act as though we know their needs better than they do.
Some evangelistic preaching tries to generate an artificial conviction of sin because the preacher feels that repentance and
forgiveness are the needs that must be faced first. They must be
faced, but sometimes they come a little later.

In an old fable, the sun and the wind had a contest to see
who could get a man to take off his coat. The wind blew harder
and harder, and the man only drew his coat closer around him.
Then the sun sent out its warmth, and in a short time the man
willingly took off his coat. Some preaching is like a cold wind
to the hearers. It makes them more defensive. Preaching that
is warm, that meets people's needs, adds motive to understanding and makes communication effective. This is why
Jesus Christ crucified is so important. A suffering Savior
evokes needs that people feel but seldom express. And when
his suffering is seen to be undeserved and for us, it gives a value
and a worth to the gospel that cannot be surpassed. It is not just
the *truth* but the *applicability* of what we say that matters.


## It's Not What They Like, but What They Do

The object of preaching the gospel is that people might turn
to God so that he can heal them (Matthew 13:15). Communica-

tion can be impressive. Rhetoric can be enjoyable. Preaching can be a blessing. We say to the pastor at the church door, "I enjoyed your message." These can be gains for which to be grateful, but they can also be dangerous. "The time will come," says Paul, "when people will . . . follow their own desires and will collect for themselves more and more teachers who will tell them what they are itching to hear" (2 Timothy 4:3, TEV). We breed "sermon-tasters" who have roast preacher every Sunday for lunch. We develop unwritten, mostly unpublished, top ten charts for preachers.

The active response that should follow preaching can be temporary or permanent. The seed that fell in good soil bore lasting fruit. That seed sown in the rocks and among thorns did not last. Jesus calls us to bear fruit that should remain (John 15:16). Whether we get a life-changing response from preaching depends on the work of the Holy Spirit. The parable of the sower, however, shows that response is affected by how well the hearers understand the message—and that hangs on effective communication.

A lady once said about her minister, "He is very nice and his sermons are most moving, but I do wish he would tell us what he wants us to do." It is not what people *like,* but what they *do* that matters.

If we as evangelists desire our seed to fall on good soil and produce a harvest of life-changing results, we need to be aware of the needs and perceptions of our hearers. Telling the gospel story is not enough; we must communicate it in a way that reaches our listeners at their point of need, that brings the Good News into focus for their lives.

*Tom Houston, former President of World Vision International, was recently named International Director of the Lausanne Committee for World Evangelization. He has also pastored Baptist churches in Kenya and Scotland. This chapter was taken from his address, "We Become All Things to All Men," delivered at the 1983 International Conference for Itinerant Evangelists in Amsterdam.*

# Chapter Four
# Equipping Ourselves for Ministry

## Brian Kingsmore

The privilege of being an evangelist is tempered by the responsibility such a high and holy calling entails. Governing all our endeavors is the sovereignty of the Holy Spirit. Only he can create anxious thoughts, change minds and attitudes, interpret truth, and give power for people to repent and turn from the world to Christ. The preaching of the gospel, then, is man's message and method *under the Holy Spirit's control.*

We need to be quite clear in our minds as to what preaching the gospel in an evangelistic campaign actually is, and above all, the primacy of the preaching in such a setting. Sometimes, for various reasons, gospel preaching has fallen into disrepute:

(a) *Attitudes differ among Christians as to the authority of Scripture.* If we do not have great authority, if we do not have great biblical themes, then we will not have great authoritative preaching.

(b) *The platform may be used for personal performance.* Some ministries are more reminiscent of the theater than of a gospel campaign. The preacher has become so professional and slick that he would not be out of place as a vaudeville act.

(c) *The content of some preaching has been very thin.* The primary task of the evangelist is to preach the gospel. We follow our Lord's example. He performed miracles, he declared prophetic truth, he led a sinless life; but his primary task was to preach the Good News. "Seek ye first the kingdom of God." "Render unto God the things that are God's."

Jesus sent out his disciples to preach and teach. All his miracles were means of directing people's attention to the Son of God who saves, and who is the Way, the Truth, and the Life. The Great Commission was to go into all the world and preach the gospel. The disciples at Pentecost were baptized with power—not for glory, but for the gospel.

That's what the early church did—preached the gospel. When a dispute arose between the Hellenistic Greek Christians and the Aramaic Christians as to the daily ministrations for the widows (Acts 6), the apostles said, "Select somebody from among yourselves; it is not seemly or desirable that we should leave the Word of God." Their priority was to the preaching of the Word and prayer.

The history of the church carried on the biblical emphasis of the supremacy of preaching. The fact that modern-day men wish to equate dialogue with preaching, or to use testimonies or group discussion or musicals in place of preaching, is only a reflection as to how far some have moved from the biblical priority of preaching. How shall they hear without a preacher?

On the evidence of Scripture and the testimony of church history, the primary task of the evangelist is to preach the gospel. Everything else in an evangelistic crusade should emphasize this priority. I believe this position to be sound theologically. Paul, at Athens, declared emphatically, "Whom therefore ye ignorantly worship, him declare I unto you" (Acts 17:23, KJV). That's the evangelistic task—declaring Christ and seeking a response.

All of us need to be fully aware of our responsibilities as evangelists. We stand before crowds of people, some large, some small, but we represent Christ. We are ambassadors for Christ.

# Doing Our Homework

The importance of our calling requires from us diligence and preparation. We need to be committed to research, to study, to an understanding of and empathy with our hearers, and to flexibility in our methods of meeting our hearers' needs.

(a) *We must know the audience makeup.* James F. Engle says that "successful communication strategy requires a sophisticated analysis and understanding of the audience if the church is to succeed in penetrating societies with the message of the gospel."

Often in my younger days, when I was invited to conduct evangelistic crusades, I pulled out of my "barrel" ten or twelve tried and tested gospel messages and went forth to "do" a crusade. In doing so, I:

- Disregarded the audience entirely. Sometimes those audiences received totally inappropriate messages in a cultural manner that was quite foreign.

- Promoted my own ideas as to what they should hear. No one sermon or group of sermons can meet the wide varieties of needs that the itinerant evangelist encounters.

- Forgot that methods of presentation often become stereotyped and outmoded. Message and method must be balanced in its preparation and presentation. If not, the message is inappropriate and the method alien at worst, hackneyed and stereotyped at best.

In today's society, such an approach will do nothing but harm to the service of evangelism. We have a responsibility in the communicating process for which we are accountable. I must know my audience and the various segments within the group; otherwise I cannot expect to prepare sermons that will meet their needs, or to preach the message in a language and style that they will understand.

To know our audience, we must "inform our minds with regard to the age, education, lifestyle, goals, activities, felt needs, problems, philosophies, and above all, the religious posture adopted by our congregation." We do not wish to prepare a message on Ecclesiastes 12:1 for a service which turns out to be packed with senior citizens; or a message about the sea to a group of landlubbers; or the blessedness of the married state to singles.

"Our audience processes the message through a perceptional filter which contains the accumulated experiences, information, values, attitudes, and other dispositions of the individual." Our audiences, in other words, screen out any unwanted messages, anything that conflicts with or is incompatible with felt needs, interests, or background. Conversely, those things with which they identify or in which they become interested are more readily admitted, because they are more compatible. Understanding audience makeup is important.

(b) *We must know the biblical message.* In order to know the message, we must spend time in researching the Bible, preparing the presentation, and timing and rehearsing, if necessary. Most of us know the Bible and the biblical constants as far as the gospel presentation is concerned. But we need to be thoroughly prepared mentally and spiritually to stand up and preach so that men and women will not dismiss Christ as irrelevant because of our lack of preparation. Men and women are either lost or saved, and they will not be saved by erroneous doctrine.

(c) *We must know the course of action.* An ancient question asks, "How will one know when he has arrived, if he does not know where he is going?" What do we want to happen as a result of our preaching the gospel? What audience response do we expect? Are we "hoping for the least," as someone recently replied? If we are hazy about procedure, if our goals are ill-defined, we will end up frustrated and ready to quit.

We need to think through what God wants by way of audience response, then employ biblical strategy to achieve that goal. We can familiarize ourselves with the layout of the hall, microphones, inquiry room, counselors, assistants, and choir. If we know how long each part of the service will take, which hymns are to be sung, the testimony to be given, we can be on top of all that is happening so that we are in the right place in the right spirit at the right time to be used by the Holy Spirit.

These *ABCs* of research require much prayer, time, and attention to detail. Evangelists must release themselves from the oft-quoted charge of thoughtlessness in the matter of gospel presentation. We must do our homework—research our subject. If we have done this adequately, then the communication process will be natural, and the truth will be conveyed with much more impact.

By knowing the local history, geography, and culture; by familiarizing ourselves with daily happenings that we hear on local radio, see on television, or read in the local press; by using thought forms and quotations that the audience identifies with; and by illustrating our biblical outlines with words and themes with which they are familiar—in such ways the main ideas of our message are driven home.

Familiarity with the audience, preparation under the guidance of the Holy Spirit, and knowledge of the procedure to be adopted give the evangelist great confidence. If the evangelist is uncertain, if he appears insecure, the chances of many hearers being convinced are reduced. The Holy Spirit does the convicting and the converting, but the preacher also conveys his own personal convictions.

## Preparing the Message

Martyn Lloyd-Jones said that two elements are vitally necessary in preaching: the correct blending of the sermon itself, and the actual act of preaching.

For the evangelist, the type of sermon is already defined. It is to be evangelistic. It is also to be simple and direct. Twentieth-century people are not hanging on our every word. Whether they are city slickers or country folks, they are much more sophisticated than we realize. They are independent, deciding to go to the crusade or not; if they do go, they decide when to turn us off or tune us in.

How we present our material is crucial. The commercial world requires simplicity in presentation. Twentieth-century evangelists must have a twentieth-century approach. Attempts to communicate in a outdated fashion result in indifference at best and resentment at worst.

## Delivering the Message

Effective evangelism *is* possible. We believe God is going to do great things in and through us, in proportion to our willingness to be used. God wants to use us as we are, not conformed to other evangelists—no matter how great. He wants us to be ourselves.

Up to now, in some measure we have been attempting a philosophy of ministry for evangelists. Our philosophy will determine not only the materials we use and present, but also how we actually do it. Do we expect, feel, believe that God will use us to lead hundreds to repentance and faith in Jesus Christ? We need to demonstrate this in our *own* way through our personality, earnestness, enthusiasm, loving, compelling presentation. If we believe the gospel story as it was, we can tell the story as it is.

It is vital that we explain our message in terms that the audience readily understands. We should use strong verbs and short sentences, and use technical terms sparingly. We shouldn't speak down to the audience, but should use nonreligious words, if possible.

We are called upon in our ministry to preach the gospel by the power of the Holy Spirit in such a way as to awaken a sense of need in the hearts and minds of those outside Christ. However, we do not rest there. We are required to point out that the needs of erring humanity are met in Jesus Christ alone. He alone is the Way, the Truth, the Life; and therefore neutrality to Jesus' claims is not possible. Our hearers need to know unmistakably that they cannot do anything to make themselves acceptable before God.

## The Invitation

At last we reach the crucial point of inviting sinners to come to Christ, to repent of their sin, and to receive by faith the gift of eternal life. How we do this is determined by our cultural standards; by the political climate of the country; by geographical location; by the numbers involved.

Where possible, I believe it is helpful for those wishing to follow Christ to indicate this publicly. Dr. Billy Graham has demonstrated by his worldwide crusades that where the Spirit moves, open public confession is possible. We must be sensitive to the local norms, but we must not be *insensitive* to the Holy Spirit's leading. Some opportunity must be given to take a definite step of faith.

Usually, the invitation comes right after the sermon's conclusion. This does not mean that prior intimation about making a decision for Christ is ruled out until the end of the message. We are preaching for a verdict, publicly demonstrated, and we need to introduce that theme early in the message.

Once the gospel invitation is given, it must be clearly understood by the hearers what is being required of them. People want to know what they have to do if they respond.

They also want to be sure, when that commitment has been taken in their hearts and minds, how to go about getting the actual transaction completed. Bringing a spiritual infant into the world is a delicate and sometimes dangerous matter.

In my own ministry, I have found certain practices helpful:

- I do not eat a large meal just before an evangelistic service.

- I need time alone with God before the service (at least thirty minutes) to prepare my heart—not the message.

- I try to preach as if it were my last sermon to people for whom it may be their last opportunity to hear the gospel. For some it is.

- I avoid criticisms and try to emphasize the "do's" rather than the "do not's."

- I do not assume anything.

- I do try to counsel at least one of the inquirers myself. In this way, that vital contact with the public is maintained.

Facing national problems of famine, moral problems, problems of backsliding, pagan worship of false gods, and immorality under the guise of religion, the prophet Hosea cried out, "O Israel, return unto the Lord thy God" (Hosea 14:1, KJV). God promised such a turning people, "I will heal their backsliding, I will love them freely" (v. 4). Ours is a high and holy calling; we need people of God to be like Hosea.

God wants to save our world. He is not looking for methods, but people who will be open to the Holy Spirit and be obedient heralds like Hosea, Peter, Paul, and many others. To all such, God has promised, "But ye shall receive power, after that the Holy Ghost is come upon you: and ye shall be witnesses unto me both in Jerusalem, and in all Judea, and in Samaria, and unto the uttermost part of the earth" (Acts 1:8, KJV).

John Wesley wrote in his journal, "I came into the town and offered them Christ." Could any work be more thrilling than that? By God's help and with the fiery earnestness of predecessors like Wesley, Whitefield, Moody, Nicholson, and Billy Graham, we will set alight the forest of error in our lands.

*Brian A. Kingsmore, a native of Belfast, Northern Ireland, has pastored three churches, served as a university chaplain, and directed evangelism outreaches in Northern Ireland. For the past five years he has directed the Evangelism and Church Growth program for Columbia Bible College and Seminary, Columbia, South Carolina. This chapter is taken from his message at the 1983 International Conference for Itinerant Evangelists in Amsterdam, and was previously published as "Message Preparation and Delivery," in* The Work of an Evangelist *(Minneapolis: World Wide Publications, 1984), 129.*

# Chapter Five
# Preparation of the Evangelistic Message

## Jim Henry

Not long ago, a lady came to me after the service, with tears streaming down her face. "Oh, I just got so blessed today," she said. "It was just wonderful!"

"Well," I said, "I'm glad you got blessed."

"I wish I could join this church," she continued, "but my husband is sick and I have to stay home with him."

"Is that right?" I asked.

"Yes, about two or three years ago he lost his mind. But he's been watching you on television and your sermons sure have meant a lot to him."

I didn't know quite how to respond, or whether it was a compliment, but I was thankful we could communicate, even though the man had lost his mind.

When I first went into the pastorate, I thought every message had to be a salvation message. I was serving in a church with about thirty or forty in worship service. The same sheep were coming every week. But, I preached every week to the lost. I wasn't feeding the sheep very much, but I certainly was telling the lost how to get saved! And then as I moved on along in my ministry, I began to realize that I needed to feed the sheep as well. And whether we're discipling believers or delivering the gospel to the lost, we need to be aware of the preparation necessary for an effective preaching ministry.

## Prepare the Preacher First

Our hearts have to be made ready, and that begins with our *devotional life*. When I get up in the morning, I read the Scriptures. I quote them when I get out of bed, and I read the Bible to get my mind focused God-ward early in the morning. I usually jog every other morning, and on that route I have thirty to fifty minutes of quiet time with God. When I don't jog, I go into the backyard, to the back bedroom, or to my church office, and have a quiet time with God. I read the Scripture, I pray, and meditate, every day, every week. If I miss it, then I find myself coming up short in my own estimation, and I don't feel prepared to preach an evangelistic message.

An evangelistic message begins with me—my personal life, my speech, my manners, my role as a husband, a father, my attitude toward the opposite sex. If I want to preach evangelistically, my *personal life* has to be right. Am I on good terms with my wife? Have we settled our arguments? Have I abused her mentally in any way? If I leave for the office at odds with my wife, I have to call home and say, "I was wrong this morning; will you forgive me?" Once I get that right, then I can prepare to preach.

My *professional life* must also be right, for me to have an effective ministry. Do I pay my bills? Do I tell the truth? Do I speak with integrity? Am I willing to take a stand on an issue on Monday face-to-face with a person, as I did on Sunday when I was safely in the pulpit where no one could confront me? Professionally, my life must be right if I want to preach evangelistic messages.

My *example* is important in my personal preparation. Dr. W. F. Powell, my first pastor, is my example for being a pastor. I don't remember one single sermon that he preached, yet the example of that man still is in my mind's eye. He came to see us and brought Double Bubble gum, when it was not easily available after World War II. He found the gum somewhere, and stopped at our little duplex; he took time out from a huge church to find two little boys and bring them bubble gum. He took time to hug me, to encourage me, to give me a Bible. And I watched him. Our lives and our examples are to be such that after we are gone, the light of our lives leaves a trail for somebody else to follow. To preach an evangelistic message, we begin with preparing the preacher.

## Prepare the Church

If there is going to be a harvest, the church has to be prepared, and it begins with my *personal example*. Is witnessing a part of my lifestyle? Do I witness in counseling, looking for an opportunity to lead people to Christ? Do I take the time each week to try to win somebody to Christ? Every Monday night I set aside as a night to visit people and try to lead them to Christ. I've had the privilege of leading scores of people to Christ in their homes on Monday and then see them respond publicly on the following Sunday.

Preparing the church includes *prayer groups*. People in our church pray for others to come to know Christ. At one time, fifteen hundred people in our church signed up to pray ten minutes a day for the church—we called it "Fifteen Hundred Praying Ten." Every week, we had hundreds of people praying to the Lord of the harvest for lost people. Currently, we have an Intercessory Prayer Room manned by our people— seven days a week, sixteen hours a day. As a result, every month we spend nearly five hundred hours in constant prayer. We started out with just a few; the number is irrelevant. If we get a group of people praying for people to come to Jesus, we can get the church prepared by prayer.

*Evangelistic efforts* are also part of preparing the church. Once every year or so, I invite men who have the gift of evangelism to lead a series of evangelistic meetings. We usually have a great harvest when those men come and minister their gifts to the church.

*Evangelism training* is another important aspect of church preparation. We need not just to preach, but to equip the saints. At my church in Nashville, I began with two women and two men and trained them with Evangelism Explosion. We started with four, and when I left the church some years later, we were training nearly a hundred and fifty people a year.

Finally, to prepare the church, we must have a *sense of spiritual growth*. People have to believe that it is a biblical priority to reach people. In our church we cancel everything on Monday nights so that people will be free to go visiting.

## Prepare to Preach

I have learned that if I don't *make preparation a priority*, I'm not going to preach much of any substance. So I clear the calendar to prepare to preach. All day Tuesday, all day Wednesday, Thursday morning, and Friday morning, unless there is an emergency, I'm in the study with the door closed preparing to preach on Sunday.

I used to go study for an hour, and then go counsel somebody, answer this phone, run down here and see Miss Jones, and go over here to see Tom and Dick, do this, run in and grab thirty minutes more study, and run out again. Finally I had to decide; if I was called to equip the saints, I'd better get in that study. I have made it a priority for about ten years now, and God has honored it. I have found more people coming to Christ, and more response when I made study a priority than I ever had when I was trying to do everything for everyone.

In preparing the message, we also need *a place for study*. I found that if I could separate my study from my administrative duties, counseling with people, answering the telephone, dictating or writing letters, and meeting with committees—I was more effective in study.

In addition to a place for study, and priority of preparation, I *protect the study*. My secretary tells people I will return their calls later. She doesn't let any call come through unless I have told her or it is an absolute emergency. I don't have people crowding out my time in the study. Protecting the study helps me prepare the message of God.

When I come to actually *preparing the message,* I first seek to know the Holy Spirit's leading. I pray, "Lord, Sunday morning people are going to be sitting out here. How do you want me to minister to them? What do you want to say to your church through this passage?" Then I bring every possible source to bear on that passage, collect illustrations, then just keep on at it until I push through with something. Whatever my subject, I try to do what Spurgeon advised: "When you find your text, wherever it is, just cut cross-country to Jesus." I try to bring that message, so that the people there know that Jesus loves them and has a claim on their lives.

## Prepare for Response

When I preach I have a *goal in mind* for hearers to respond to. I believe God has given me the gift of exhortation. What am I exhorting them to do? When I give an invitation, and I preach to Christians, what am I expecting that person in the pew to do out there? That business man? The housewife? The career woman? The single person? I try to make my invitation correspond to the message I preach. If we preach to human problems, that Jesus Christ and the Word of God can minister to them, he uses that point of contact to lead in people's lives and bring them to a confession of faith in him.

One year at the holiday season, we had a "singing Christmas tree." We had about a hundred people up on a Christmas tree singing the music of Christmas. At the end, a cross came up in lights, and the choir sang, "There's Room at the Cross for You."

I stepped out on the stage and told a little story as they sang the gospel, and then I said, "Some of you here tonight may have never asked Jesus to come into your heart. Maybe you never knew how to pray, and so I'm going to lead you in a prayer. Most of you are familiar with the sinner's prayer, so just pray this prayer to God with me."

There were two thousand people there; I was up on the platform, and I began to pray, "Dear Lord . . ."

And I heard someone say, "Dear Lord . . ."

"Tonight . . ."

"Tonight . . ."

"I realize I am a sinner . . ."

"I realize I am a sinner . . ."

At first I thought it was a problem with feedback in the speakers. Then I realized that a guy in the balcony was praying the prayer with me—out loud, in front of two thousand people! Electricity ran through that room; everybody realized what was happening. As I was praying, his voice began to get louder, and he began to cry. He accepted Jesus, and just broke out into weeping. In front of two thousand people he made a very public confession of faith.

When it was over the people surrounded him. We found out later that he had been an agnostic, and had come with some friends who had been praying for him for a long time. He had come under duress, to please his friends, yet the Holy Spirit had spoken to him during the performance that night. Nonetheless, had I not given the invitation, I can't be sure that he would have actually come to Jesus, except for the sovereignty of God.

When we are prepared for evangelism—prepared in personal ways, prepared for preaching, and prepared for response, we are ready to be used of God in people's lives. They will be drawn to him, and we will have the joy of reaping the bountiful harvest.

*James B. Henry has served churches in Alabama, Mississippi, and Tennessee, and since 1977 has been pastor of First Baptist Church, Orlando, Florida. He has held many denominational positions, including president of the SBC Pastors Conference (1981) and trustee of the Foreign Mission Board (1978-88). He is a frequent guest speaker on college campuses, at conferences, and on television. This chapter is taken from his message, "Preparation for Evangelistic Preaching," given at the Billy Graham School of Evangelism, Hartford, Connecticut, May 1985.*

# Chapter Six
# Setting Forth the Truth Plainly

## *Billy Graham*

The well-known German theologian Rudolph Bultmann has asked the right question for our age: "How do we communicate the gospel in a secularistic and technological age?" This question might be put differently in different cultures, but all of us are concerned with effectively communicating the gospel. In many circumstances it means what missiologists have called "contextualization"—we adapt our methods to the culture and society in which we are called to proclaim the gospel. But we have no authority from Scripture to alter the *message*. The message can never be contextualized.

Thus this question arises again: How do we communicate the gospel with power and effect in this materialistic, scientific, rebellious, secular, immoral, humanistic age?

## The Key

The key to effective gospel communication is found in 1 Corinthians 2:2: "For I resolved to know nothing while I was with you except Jesus Christ and him crucified."

When Paul went to Corinth, it was one of the most idolatrous, pagan, intellectual, and immoral cities in all of the Roman world. If you wanted to condemn someone as an immoral person, you called him a "Corinthian." When Paul looked at this city, and felt God's leadership to start a church there, what did he do? How could he communicate in that place? There was not a single other Christian in town—not even a Baptist! Paul was the only believer. What would he do? How could he "preach the gospel" in an atmosphere alien to its very nature? That is always the question. It is the prime question today.

If we could ask Paul personally those searching questions, perhaps he would respond, "My intelligence alone will not be able to handle it. I do not have the logic or the arguments to compel the Corinthians to accept the truth of the gospel." What, then, did he do? He said, with positive faith, "For I resolved to know nothing while I was with you except Jesus Christ and him crucified." Paul knew that there was a "built-in" power in the Cross; it has its own communicative power. Paul knew that the Holy Spirit takes the simple message of the Cross, with its message of love and grace, through the proclaiming of Christ, and infuses it into lives with authority and power.

Furthermore, the Spirit's work is vital, for, "The man without the Spirit does not accept the things that come from the Spirit of God, for they are foolishness to him, and he cannot understand them, because they are spiritually discerned" (1 Corinthians 2:14).

Therefore, when we proclaim the *kerygma* (as Paul describes it in 1 Corinthians 15), when we preach Christ crucified, there's a power—dynamite—in it. Proclaimers of the gospel must *always* realize, as Paul stressed, that the natural man simply cannot accept the truth of Christ unless the veil is lifted by the Holy Spirit.

But the marvelous fact is, the Holy Spirit takes the message and communicates it with power to the heart and mind, breaking down every barrier. It's a supernatural act of the Spirit of God. No evangelist can have God's touch on his ministry until he realizes these realities and preaches in the power of the Holy Spirit. In the final analysis, the Holy Spirit is the communicator.

## Some Safe Assumptions

When I go out and proclaim the gospel, in every congregation, and any group—whether it's on a street corner in Nairobi, in a meeting in Seoul, Korea, in a tribal situation in Zaire, or in a large stadium in New York City—I know that certain things are true in the hearts and minds of all people, that certain psychological and spiritual factors exist in everyone. As I begin to communicate, I can trust the Holy Spirit to strike certain responsive chords in every human heart that hears:

(a) *Life's needs are not totally met by social improvement or material affluence.* This is true around the world and in every culture. Jesus said, "A man's life does not consist in the abundance of his possessions" (Luke 12:15).

(b) *There is an essential "emptiness" in every life without Christ.* All humanity keeps crying for something; something—they do not know what it is. Give a person a million dollars—it doesn't satisfy. Or give him sex and every form of sensuality; that too never satisfies the deep longing inside that keeps crying for satisfaction. One of the male sex symbols of America said, "I've slept with some of the most beautiful women in the world. But it doesn't bring fulfillment and peace. I'm one of the most miserable men in the world." There is another level to life. We can assume that truth as we preach Christ in the power of the Holy Spirit.

In our universities, young people are intellectually, psychologically, and spiritually lost. They are searching for something, and they don't know what it is. Dr. Derek Bok, president of Harvard University, said that the greatest lack among the students was commitment. Pascal described the "God-shaped vacuum" in every life that only God can fill. When we proclaim the gospel, we're talking directly to that emptiness. The person with whom you're communicating, whether in personal witnessing or before a group, has a "built-in" receptivity to the message of the Cross, because Christ alone fills the void.

(c) *Our hearers face loneliness.* Some have called it "cosmic loneliness." A psychiatrist and theologian at an American university was asked, "What is the greatest problem of the patients that come to you for help?" He thought for a moment and responded, "Loneliness." He went on, "When you get right down to it, it is a loneliness for God." We all sense something of that. You can be in a crowd of people, even at a party, and suddenly, with all the people around laughing, a loneliness will sweep over you—just for a moment. That "cosmic loneliness" is everywhere: loneliness in the suburbs, loneliness in the ghettos, loneliness in Africa, loneliness in Latin America, loneliness in Japan. It is a loneliness that only God can fill.

(d) *People have a sense of guilt.* Guilt is perhaps the most universal of all human experiences, and it is devastating. The head of a mental institution in London said, "I could release half of my patients if I could but find a way to rid them of their sense of guilt." What a tremendously relevant message we have for that problem! This is what the Cross is all about. When we preach Christ, we are speaking directly to the nagging, depressing problem of guilt. And that problem is always there. We don't make people feel guilty, they already do. We tell them what the guilt is. We tell them it is rebellion against God, and we tell them the Cross is the answer!

(e) *People have a fear of death.* We do not like to talk about death in our generation. But death is real. We can turn on the television and see movie stars such as Marilyn Monroe or Clark Gable; they look alive, but they are dead. Somehow television, especially in Western society, has cushioned death. Yet the specter is always there. The subtle fear cannot be silenced. But here is the glorious news: Our Lord came to nullify death. In his own death and resurrection, he made three things inoperative: sin, death, and hell. That's the message of the Cross.

## Principles of Communicating the Gospel

All these assumptions can be realized as we preach Christ. The Holy Spirit will apply the message to these deep-seated needs. But now the question is: In the midst of all these assumptions, how are we to communicate the gospel?

(a) *We communicate the gospel with authority.* We need to preach with assurance, remembering that "faith comes from hearing the message, and the message is heard through the word of Christ" (Romans 10:17). My one criticism of modern theological education is that we are not putting enough emphasis on authoritative preaching. Where are the great preachers today—the Luthers, the Calvins, the Knoxes, the Spurgeons? Churches are constantly asking for recommendations for pastors, and they all say, "In our particular situation, we have to have somebody who can preach." But where are the preachers that speak with confidence and authority? At conferences, we always see the same names: men who can preach authoritatively. But how do we learn to communicate with such power?

In my early days, when I started to prepare a sermon, I got a book of sermons by a famous Texan preacher. I took two of his sermons, along with a couple of his outlines, and I would preach them out loud ten to twenty times. In my first sermon, in Bostic, Florida, at the Baptist church, I was trembling. I had prepared four sermons. I practiced as I described, until I knew that each one of them would last forty minutes. I got up and preached all four in eight minutes! It takes hard work to prepare effective messages. We must saturate ourselves in the Word of God, get to the place where we can say, as Spurgeon said of Psalm 119, "Oh, the depths." We need to pray and pray until we *know* we have God's message, until we are sure his divine anointing is on us.

Dr. Sid Bonnell said to his class at Princeton, "If you are preaching under the anointing of the Holy Spirit, the hearers will hear another 'Voice.'" Are people conscious of that other "Voice" when we preach? Are we Spirit-filled (Ephesians 5:18)? Do we preach with God's authority? His authority is absolutely essential to the communication of the gospel. One reason the people listened to Jesus was that he spoke as one having authority.

We need to preach with authority. When we quote God's Word, he will use it. He will never allow it to return void.

One day my wife was in the famous London bookstore, Foyles. A fellow came out, discouraged and despondent. He said to my wife, "You look like a real Christian. My family's torn up. I'm on the verge of suicide."

She asked, "Well, why not go out to the Harringay Arena tonight and hear Billy Graham?"

"Oh," he said, "I don't think he could help me, I'm beyond help." But she gave him some tickets, and he came.

The next year, when we were at Wembley Stadium, she went back to Foyles. That same little fellow came running out. He said, "Oh, Mrs. Graham, that night I went to Harringay and I was converted to Christ. And I'm the happiest person in Britain!" He went on, "The verse your husband preached on that night that God saved me was a verse from the Psalms, 'I am like a pelican of the wilderness: I am like an owl of the desert'" (Psalm 102:6, KJV).

My wife scratched her head. "I never thought of that as a gospel verse."

"That verse described me completely," he said, "and I was saved."

God uses his Word. His power is in the Word.

(b) *We preach the gospel with simplicity.* Dr. James S. Stewart, of Edinburgh, said, "You never preach the gospel unless you preach it with simplicity. If you shoot over the heads of your hearers, you don't prove anything except you have a poor aim." We must learn to take the profoundest things of God and proclaim them with simplicity.

In our Berlin Congress on Evangelism in 1966, one of the papers read by an American theologian was deep and involved. Many of the Christians really did not understand what he was talking about. An African in his native dress had not been able to make out a thing that the learned professor said. But he went right up and hugged the speaker and kissed him in front of everybody, and he said, "You know, I don't understand a thing you say, but I'm so glad that a man who knows as much as you know is on our side." The sentiment was touching, but we must communicate so that people understand as well.

I have a friend on the West Coast, a minister in the Methodist Church. One Sunday before the worship hour, he decided he was going to present some visual education for the children.

He decided he would preach his children's sermon with all sorts of slides he had made during the week. This, he thought, would illustrate his simple sermon and help the children to understand. To his amazement he found that the older people began to come early until the church was packed to hear his children's sermons, and the attendance at his eleven o'clock worship service was dropping. He had made a grand discovery: The more simple he made his communication, the more people came to hear. People want simplicity. I am sure that was one of the secrets of the ministry of our Lord. The Bible says, "The common people heard him gladly" (Mark 12:37, KJV). Why? For one central reason. They understood him. He spoke their language.

(c) *We preach with repetition.* Professor James Denney, of Glasgow, once said that Jesus probably repeated himself more than five hundred times. That is an encouragement to every evangelist. The gospel may at times seem "old" to us. But it is "news" to multitudes. We must never tire, and never be embarrassed to share the news over and over again.

(d) *We preach with urgency; we preach for a decision.* People are dying. We may be speaking to some who will hear the gospel for the last time. We must preach with the urgency of Christ, preach it to bring our hearers to Christ, preach for decision, preach for a verdict, as Jesus did. The call to repentance and faith is part of the proclamation, too.

(e) *We are to communicate the gospel by a holy life.* Our world today is looking primarily for men and women of integrity, communicators who back up their ministry with their lives. Our preaching emerges out of what we are. We *must* be a holy people. Those who have affected me most profoundly have not been the great orators, but holy men and women. That is where the emphasis must be placed. Robert Murray McCheyne said, "A holy man is an awful weapon in God's hand." Paul said, "I keep under my body, and bring it into subjection" (1 Corinthians 9:27, KJV).

There are three avenues through which the Devil attacks young evangelists (and older preachers too): money, morals, and pride. As evangelists, we will battle with all three all our lives. We must be ready; the Devil will set traps for us constantly.

When we first started in evangelism, Cliff Barrows and I determined that we were going to incorporate and have a board, and pay ourselves a set salary. It caused a furor. Some said, "You're going to ruin evangelism." But I believe that God has honored the way we've handled the finances. We must never bring reproach on evangelism over money. Evangelists are so vulnerable where finances are concerned. We must be holy.

This holiness is not merely negative—"don't do this, or, don't do that." It is positive. We must immerse ourselves in the Word of God. We must be a people of prayer. A disciplined devotional life is vital to holy living.

(f) _We communicate the gospel by our love of people._ "All men will know that you are my disciples, if you love one another" (John 13:35). A layman in Boston went boldly into a hotel, walked up to a lady, and said, "Do you know Christ?"

When she told her husband about it, he said, "Didn't you tell him to mind his own business?"

She replied, "But, my dear, if you'd seen the expression on his face and heard the earnestness with which he spoke, you would have thought it _was_ his business."

When we speak to people about Christ, personally or in preaching, do they think that it is our business? Do we really love people? Does it show? Do they sense our compassion?

One of our associate evangelists was preaching in Central America at the university on one occasion. He tried to win the students to Christ, and they showed him a great deal of hostility. One student was especially hostile. After the service, this intelligent young woman, working on her doctoral degree, came up to him and said, "I don't believe any of that hogwash."

He responded, "Well, I don't think I agree; but do you mind if I pray for you?"

"No one ever prayed for me before," she replied. "I don't guess it will do any harm." He bowed his head, but she looked straight ahead and was defiant when he started to pray. As he prayed for the conversion of that girl, the tears began to flow down his cheeks. When he opened his eyes, she was broken up with tears and said, "No one in my whole life has loved me enough to shed a tear for me." They sat down on a bench, and that girl accepted the Lord as her Savior. How many of us have loved so much that we have shed tears?

(g) *We communicate the gospel by a compassionate social concern.* People ask me, "Billy, do you believe in the social gospel?" Of course I do. I believe that social involvement is commanded in the Scripture. Our Lord touched the leper. That leper, ostracized forever until his death, had to cry constantly, "Unclean! Unclean!" Yet Jesus touched him. Jesus was teaching by example as well as precept that we have a responsibility to the oppressed, the sick, the poor (Luke 4:18–19).

I was told by one of our economic experts, "We're one crop away from a massive world famine that will affect even the United States." The world is headed toward a gigantic crisis of food. Are we concerned? Our Association sends thousands of dollars each year to help. Yes, I believe in a "social gospel." I love people. We are to have a compassionate social concern.

We all have to admit that many of us have not done our share—we have not done enough. We have too often been silent in the face of critical social issues. But it is also wrong to condemn all evangelicals as having little or no social concern. We have only to think of historical figures like John Wesley, Charles Finney, William Booth, Jonathan Blanchard (the founder of Wheaton College, which has been called the "Harvard" of evangelical education), or Martin Luther King, Jr. (who came from an evangelical background).

For two or three generations, when the so-called fundamentalist-modernist controversy was raging in the early 1920s, the reaction by certain groups (even foreign missionary organizations) against the so-called "social gospel" became so great that they pulled into a shell and gave the evangelical movement a bad reputation concerning social involvement. But in the past few years, a drastic change has been taking place; and evangelicals in many parts of the world are in the forefront of social change. In Nigeria, for example, four thousand schools have been established by people who are motivated by the gospel of

Jesus Christ.

But the church goes into the world with an extra dimension to its social concern. We go in the name of our Lord Jesus Christ. We reach out to meet needs and give, but we must always say, "Given in the name of our Lord Jesus Christ." That is our motivation. And we can often use that means as a vehicle that they can see Christ in us. Therefore, it never becomes mere humanitarianism. We give because God gave.

When I met the former Prime Minister of Britain, Harold Wilson, he shook hands with me and said, "Oh, yes, we come by your way." I knew what he meant. Keir Hardie, who helped found the British Labour Party, had been profoundly influenced by the ministry of evangelist Dwight L. Moody. Keir Hardie was an evangelist all his life, as well as having been deeply involved in helping and organizing the working poor. He founded the British Labour Party because of his social concern, out of love for Christ. And Prime Minister Wilson was a member of that British Labour Party.

When Martin Luther King, Jr. accepted his Nobel Peace Prize, they asked him, "Where do you get your motivation?" He said, "From my father's evangelical preaching."

(h) *We communicate the gospel by our unity in the Spirit.* If we can stay unified, yet also realize that there is diversity in unity, we can turn the world upside down for Christ. We have the instruments in our hands right now to evangelize the world before the end of this century. For the first time in the history of the Christian church, the possibility of fulfilling the Great Commission is in our grasp. But we must all work together in the "unity of the Spirit through the bond of peace" (Ephesians 4:3). This is our task, and this is our job.

*This chapter is taken from Dr. Graham's message, "We Set Forth the Truth Plainly," delivered at the 1983 International Conference for Itinerant Evangelists in Amsterdam.*

# Chapter Seven
# Focusing the Message

*Robert E. Coleman*

Evangelistic preaching is the proclamation of the gospel in the power of the Holy Spirit with the aim of making disciples for Christ. To be sure, all Christian preaching should expect a response in both faith and action, whether the sermon is a declaration of the facts of personal redemption or the teaching of some great moral truth. But in the more specialized sense, evangelistic preaching concerns the immediate message of salvation, a message that carries with it the imperative that all persons must repent and believe the gospel. Such preaching is not necessarily any special type of sermon or homiletical method; rather, it is preaching distinguished by the call for commitment to the Son of God who loved us and gave himself for us.

Preparing and delivering such a message is a holy task, and calls forth every resource of mind and spirit that God has given. Though the provisions for fulfilling the work are all of grace, this does not take away the responsibility of the preacher for observing basic rules of effective sermon building. Thus the following nine principles are most crucial.

## Pray It Through

The place to begin in sermon preparation is on our knees. Here, in renewal of our faith and our calling, totally submitted to the lordship of Christ, we are in a position to receive strength and wisdom for the message. Before we can get direction in what to tell others, we will have to hear what God has to say about correcting some deficiencies in our own lives, and confess the sin. Only when our vessel is clean are we fit for the Master's use (2 Timothy 2:21).

With a heart in tune with the will of God, we can then project our thoughts to the persons to whom we will be speaking, trying to be sensitive to their needs. A message that hits home must meet people where they are, both in their interests and attitudes concerning the subject of the sermon, as well as in their feelings toward the preacher. By knowing the nature of the audience, understanding where they are coming from, the evangelist can make the appeal more direct and meaningful in their situation.

As the burden of the message and its structure takes form, it is prayed over and presented unto God as an offering of devotion. There is a sense in which it is preached to God before anyone else. Only after the sermon has his approval can the evangelist be confident in proclaiming it to the people.

The spirit of prayer continues on through delivery. This communication with heaven makes the sermon "mighty through God to the pulling down of strong holds" (2 Corinthians 10:4, KJV). As J. Sidlow Baxter has put it, "Men may spurn our appeals, reject our message, oppose our arguments, despise our persons—but they are helpless against our prayers."[1] Prayer is evangelism in its most basic expression. To paraphrase the words of Dr. Lewis Sperry Chafer, "Winning souls is more a work of pleading for them than a service of pleading with them."[2]

---

[1] J. Sidlow Baxter, quoted in Cameron V. Thompson, *Master Secrets of Prayer* (Lincoln, Nebr.: Back to the Bible, 1959), 4.

[2] Lewis Sperry Chafer, *True Evangelism* (Grand Rapids, Mich.: Zondervan, 1919), 93.

# Lift Up Jesus

The evangelistic message itself, whatever its style, will center in Jesus Christ (Acts 5:42; 1 Corinthians 1:23; 2 Corinthians 4:5), "the fulness of the Godhead bodily" (Colossians 2:9, KJV). He is the Evangel, "the Good News" incarnate, "the Lamb of God, which taketh away the sin of the world" (John 1:29, KJV). In him every redemptive truth begins and ends. "There is none other name under heaven given among men, whereby we must be saved" (Acts 4:12, KJV). Unless people see him, regardless of what else impresses them, they will not be drawn to God.

The Revelation reaches its climax at the blood-red hill of Calvary. There nearly two thousand years ago, Jesus bore our sins in his own body on the cross, suffering in our stead, "the just for the unjust, that he might bring us to God" (1 Peter 3:18, KJV). Though any interpretation of his sacrifice falls short of its full meaning, clearly Christ, by offering himself, once and for all, made a perfect and complete atonement for the sins of the world.

Here lies the wonder of the gospel. "God commendeth his love toward us, in that, while we were yet sinners, Christ died for us" (Romans 5:8, KJV). Jesus paid it all. Nothing deserved! Nothing earned! In our complete helplessness, bankrupt of all natural goodness, he did for us what we could never do for ourselves.

His bodily resurrection and ascension into heaven brings the Cross forcibly to attention. For when one dies, who has the power to rise from the grave? In all honesty we must ask why he died in the first place. To this penetrating question, the evangelist declares: He died for you, and was raised for your salvation (Romans 4:24–25).

The whole message, then, turns on what is done with Jesus (Acts 17:30–31). Keenly aware of this, the evangelist must seek to bring into focus the person and work of the Savior. It matters little what the people think of the preacher; everything depends upon what they believe about Christ. That is why the measure of a sermon's power is the degree to which it exalts the Lord and makes the audience aware of his claims upon their lives. With this in mind, listening to the remarks of people after a preaching service is very interesting. If they talk more about the preacher than about Jesus, the sermon may have missed the mark.

## Use the Scripture

Preaching that brings people to the Savior reflects the spirit and letter of God-breathed Scripture. The word written in the Book discloses Christ the Living Word (John 20:31). It is the means by which the mind is illuminated (2 Timothy 3:16), faith is kindled (Romans 10:17), and the heart is recreated according to the purpose of God (John 17:17; 1 Peter 1:23; 2 Peter 1:4). For this reason, the redemptive power of any sermon relates directly to the way one uses the immutable, inerrant, and life-changing Word of God.

This Book is the "sword of the Spirit" in the preacher's hand (Ephesians 6:17). It gives authority to the message. Without its sure testimony, the sermon would be little more than a statement of human experience. Of course, the preacher must support the message by clear personal witness, but the ultimate authority for what is preached must be the written Word. Experience can be trusted only when it accords with the inspired Scriptures.

Thus the evangelist is commissioned simply to "preach the Word" (2 Timothy 4:2). As an ambassador of the King of heaven, he is not called to validate the message, nor to speculate or argue about conflicting opinions on the subject. God has spoken and the message permeated with this conviction is an inexorable declaration: "Thus saith the Lord!" Such preaching needs neither defense nor explanation. The Spirit of God who gave the Word will bear witness to its truthfulness (2 Peter 1:21; 1 John 5:6), and he will not let it return unto him void (Isaiah 55:11).

This is exemplified in the preaching of Billy Graham. However, there was a time in his early ministry when this confidence was missing, and he had to duel with doubts about the Bible's integrity. The struggle came to a head one evening in 1949, when alone in the mountains of California, he knelt before the open Bible, and said:

> Here and now, by faith, I accept the Bible as Thy Word. I take it all. I take it without reservations. Where there are things I cannot understand, I will reserve judgment until I receive more light. If this pleases Thee, give me authority as I proclaim Thy Word, and through that authority convict me of sin and turn sinners to their Savior.[3]

Within weeks, the Los Angeles Crusade started. There his preaching began to manifest a new power, as he quit trying to prove the Scripture, and simply declared the truth. Over and over again, he heard himself saying, "The Bible says. . . ." He said, "I felt as though I were merely a voice through which the Holy Spirit was speaking."

It was a new discovery for the young evangelist. He found that people were not especially interested in his ideas, nor were they drawn to moving oratory. They were hungry, "to hear what God had to say through his Holy Word."

This is a lesson every preacher must learn. And until it is reflected in our sermons, not much that we say is likely to generate faith in the hearts of hearers.

## Dig Out Sin

Under the refining light of the Word of God, the evangelist's message makes people face themselves before the Cross. The cloak of self-righteousness is pulled away (John 15:22), showing the deceitfulness of sin. The pretense of living independently from God is seen for what it is, the creature actually holding the will of the Creator with contempt, worshiping his own works as a false god (Romans 1:25). Its ultimate expression comes in the defiant rejection of Jesus Christ, the promised

---

[3] Billy Graham, "Biblical Authority in Evangelism," *Christianity Today* (October 15, 1956), 6.

Messiah. "He came unto his own, and his own received him not" (John 1:11, KJV).

Such blasphemy cannot be ignored by a just God, because it is an affront to his holiness and justice. Inevitably, then, the profane must be separated from him. Furthermore, his wrath upon iniquity cannot be annulled as long as the cause of evil remains. Since life is unending, all the spiritual consequences of sin continue on forever in hell.

Knowing, therefore, the terror of the Lord, the evangelist strikes at the heart of sin. Urging at one time the greatness of the rebel's guilt and at another the imminence of his doom, he seeks to awaken the human conscience. The awfulness of sin becomes vivid. Although all the diverse kinds of sin cannot be treated in one sermon, at least the basic issue of unbelief and disobedience can be disclosed, with perhaps a few specific applications to the local situation.

There should never be any confusion about whom the evangelist is addressing. It is not sin in theory but the sinner in practice that he is talking about. Indeed, it might well seem to the sinner that the preacher has been following him around all week, noting every wrong deed and thought. While, of course, considerations of propriety and good sense must be kept in mind, a sermon still must get under a person's skin and make him squirm under conviction of sin. A message that does not deal with this cause of all human woe, individually and collectively, is irrelevant to human need. Though the tragedy of rebellion and its result may be bad news, still the gospel shines through, for God judges that he might save. One thing is certain: If people do not recognize their problem, they will not want the remedy.

## Keep to the Point

The evangelistic sermon is based on a convincing course of reason. Notwithstanding the fad of irrational thinking among some existentialist ministers, consistency is still a mark of truth, and a gospel sermon should reflect this character.

For this to happen, the objective of the message must be perfectly clear. The preacher should ask himself, "What do I want to get across?" Then he should try to visualize the response expected. Unless the evangelist knows what he is aiming for, almost certainly no one else will catch on. As an exercise, it may be helpful to write out the objective in a sentence. With the goal in mind, then the evangelist can plan how to get there.

Whatever the structure of the message, a good, balanced outline will go a long way toward keeping it on course. The points should flow effortlessly out of the passage. Moreover, they should be arranged in such a way that each builds upon the other, creating a progression of thought leading up to the appeal for decision. When this is done well, the invitation seems as natural as it is necessary.

Brevity is important. The rule is to include nothing in the sermon that can be excluded. Wise counsel was given by John Wesley when he told his preachers: "Take care not to ramble, but keep to the text, and make out what you take in hand."[4]

Illustrations and human interest stories can be used as needed to clarify or to make more impressive an idea. Yet we should keep in mind that the strength of the sermon does not rest in the illustrative material. People like stories, and interest in the sermon must be sustained; but more important is the logic of the truth presented.

## Make It Simple

A well-prepared sermon will be uncomplicated in its basic organization and language (2 Corinthians 11:3). Truth when reduced to its highest expression is always simple. Anybody can make the gospel difficult to comprehend, but the person of wisdom says it so that a child can understand. Some preachers feign intellectual superiority by sermonizing in high-sounding philosophic terms, as if the message needed to be sophisticated

---

[4]John Wesley, *Methodist Discipline* (n. p., 1784), 19.

in order to appeal to the well-educated. That some clerics labor under this illusion may partially explain why so many people, including university students, scorn the church. Whenever a theological discourse gets so complicated that only a college graduate can understand it, then something is wrong, either with the theology or with its presentation.

The admonition is to speak "in simplicity and godly sincerity, not with fleshly wisdom, but by the grace of God" (2 Corinthians 1:12, KJV). Paul, probably the most astute theologian of the church, expressed the ideal when he wrote: "My speech and my preaching was not with enticing words of man's wisdom, but in demonstration of the Spirit and of power: That your faith should not stand in the wisdom of men, but in the power of God" (1 Corinthians 2:4–5, KJV).

Plain language and familiar terms will help accomplish this. Not that everything in the message can be given in an easy explanation; much that is revealed by God remains a mystery, such as the nature of the Trinity, the Incarnation, or the miraculous work of the Holy Spirit. But when the gospel of salvation is stated plainly as a fact, it makes sense to the honest soul seeking after God.

This is what counts. The evangelist does not need to answer all the curious problems of theology, but he must have an unequivocal answer to the fundamental question of perishing men and women: What must I do to be saved? One way to practice this counsel is to preach the sermon first to some ordinary wayfarers on a street corner. If they can understand it, then you can be reasonably sure that persons settled in a comfortable pew will get the point.

## Plead for Souls

The evangelist is not content merely to state the gospel; he expects people to be changed by it. The sermon thus becomes a plea in the name of Christ that persons be "reconciled to God" (2 Corinthians 5:20, KJV). A living, personal, certain experience of saving grace is the aim of the message. Definitions of that experience are not nearly so important as its reality. Without quibbling over terms, the preacher directs the sinner to the mercy seat, where by faith redemption can be found in the precious blood of the Lamb.

This keeps the sermon from becoming merely a pious statement of orthodoxy. To be sure, the message must be sound in doctrine. But its orthodoxy must be clothed with the brokenness of a preacher who knows that except for the grace of God he would be as those who have no hope. Humbled by this knowledge, the evangelist cannot be judgmental and brazen in pronouncements against others. Rather, he enters into their sorrows with compassion wrung from his own deep experience with God, and the sermon reflects this in a tenderness that the hearer is quick to recognize.

There is a vicariousness about preaching, expressing itself supremely in the yearning that all people might come and drink freely from the same fountain of Living Water that has satisfied the evangelist's own soul. This passion for persons of every race and culture to partake of divine grace, and experience for themselves a new life in Christ, is what makes an evangelistic sermon consistent with its mission.

A few years after the death of the famous preacher, Robert Murray McCheyne, a young minister visited his church to discover, as he explained, the secret of the man's amazing influence. The beadle (sexton), who had served under Mr. McCheyne, took the youthful inquirer into the vestry, and asked him to sit in the chair used by the great preacher.

"Now put your elbows on the table," he said. "Now put your face in your hands." The visitor obeyed. "Now let the tears flow! That was the way Mr. McCheyne used to do!"

The man then led the minister to the pulpit and gave him a fresh series of instructions. "Put your elbows down on the pulpit!" He put his elbows down. "Now put your face in your hands!" He did as he was told. "Now let the tears flow! That was the way Mr. McCheyne used to do!"[5]

Yes, that is the way to do it. Not that physical tears must fall,

---

[5]F. W. Boreham, *A Late Lark Singing* (London: Epworth Press, 1945), 66.

but that the compassion which they represent should characterize every preacher feeling the weight of lost souls, knowing that their destiny may hang upon his sermon.

## Call for a Verdict

The decision makes the difference. If the will is not moved to action, there can be no salvation (Romans 10:13). The truth of the message, thus, is saved from degenerating into mere rationalism on the one hand and mere emotionalism on the other by linking it with a personal response. To stir people to great aspirations without also giving them something that they can do about it leaves them worse off than they were before. They will likely become either more confused in their thinking, or more indifferent in their will. Consequently, once the gospel is made clear, the evangelist must call to account each person who hears the message. So far as he knows, this may be their last opportunity to respond.

With this burden, the evangelist cries out almost with a sense of desperation. Tremendous issues are at stake. Immortal souls are perishing in sin. Judgment is certain. God offers mercy through the blood of his Son. All must repent and believe the gospel. Heaven and hell are in the balance. Time is running out. "Behold, now is the day of salvation" (2 Corinthians 6:2, KJV).

Preaching that does not focus on the immediacy of the decision lacks evangelistic relevance. The gospel does not permit people the luxury of indecision. In the presence of the crucified and living King of Kings, one cannot be neutral. To deliberately ignore Christ is to live in a state of blasphemy, refusing forgiveness; it is to close the door to the only way of life, and life abundant.

To some persons, this assertion seems arrogant. A man once said to Dr. R. A. Torrey, "I'm not a Christian, but I am moral and upright. I would like to know what you have against me." Torrey looked the man in the eye, and replied: "I charge you, sir, with treason against heaven's King."

That is the issue which must be faced. It is not finally our gospel, but his. And because Jesus Christ is Lord, before him every knee must bow.

In this obeisance, therefore, the evangelist seeks to "persuade men" (2 Corinthians 5:11, KJV). "Whosoever will" may come (Revelation 22:17, KJV). He cannot make the decision for anyone, but as God leads, he is responsible for doing what he can to make the issues clear. Eternal destinies are at stake.

## Depend on the Holy Spirit

One final ingredient must be understood about evangelistic preaching, apart from which everything said thus far would be as a sounding brass and tinkling cymbal: The Spirit of God must have control. Throughout the sermon presentation, delivery, and invitation, he is the divine enabler. Preaching the gospel, as any Christian work, is not contrived by human ingenuity. All we can do is to make ourselves available for the Spirit to use. Failure to appreciate this truth, I suspect, is the reason so many sermons fall flat.

The third person of the Trinity effects in and through us what Christ has done for us. It is the Spirit who gives life; the flesh profits nothing (John 6:63). He initiates and guides prayer. He lifts up the Son, thereby drawing persons to the Father. He makes the inspired Scripture come alive. He convicts of sin, of righteousness, and of judgment. He guides the obedient servant into truth, making the message clear to seeking hearts. He recreates and sanctifies through the Word. And he extends the call for weary and heavy laden souls to come to Jesus. From beginning to end, the whole enterprise of evangelism is in the authority and demonstration of God's Spirit.

We can understand, then, why the glorified Savior told his disciples to tarry until they be filled with his Spirit (Luke 24:49; Acts 1:4–5,8). How else could they fulfill their mission? The word and work of their Lord had to become a burning compulsion within them. The superhuman ministry to which they were called required supernatural help—an enduement of power from on high.

This is nowhere more necessary than with gospel preachers. Any sermon that circumvents this provision will be as lifeless as it is barren. So let us trust him. As God has called us into his harvest, he will provide what is needed to do the work. The secret of evangelism, finally, is to let the Holy Spirit have his way.

This then is the task of preparing and delivering an evangelistic message: Pray the sermon through; lift up Jesus and his saving work; use the authority of Scripture; come to grips with sin; keep the logic of the message clear; make the presentation simple; plead with compassion for persons to experience the Savior; call for a decision; and wait upon the Holy Spirit of God. Such preaching will shake the gates of hell, and make the courts of heaven reverberate with shouts of glory.

One January day in 1930, Walter Vivian of CBS was checking the equipment which had been installed to carry the message of King George V to the British navy around the world. In a last-minute inspection, Vivian discovered a break in the wires. There was no time for it to be repaired. So grasping the two segments of the wire—each with a hand—he became the conductor through which 220 volts of electricity passed. He came out of the experience with burned hands, but the king's message was transmitted to the ends of the earth.[6] So may it be with us in transmitting the message of the King of heaven. Whatever it takes, wherever we may be placed in his service, let us become a conductor through which the Spirit of God can bring the Good News of Jesus Christ to every creature.

*Robert E. Coleman is Professor of Evangelism, as well as Director of the School of World Mission and Evangelism and Chairman of the Department of Mission and Evangelism at Trinity Evangelical Divinity School in Deerfield, Illinois. He is also Director of the Billy Graham Institute of Evangelism at Wheaton College. He is author of*

---

[6]Lloyd Merle Perry, "Preaching for Decision," in *Evangelism on the Cutting Edge*, ed. Robert E. Coleman, (Old Tappan, N.J.: Fleming H. Revell, 1986), 124.

*nineteen books, including* Master Plan of Evangelism, *and* The Spark That Ignites, *published by World Wide Publications. This chapter is taken from his message, "Preparing and Delivering an Evangelistic Message," presented at the 1986 International Conference for Itinerant Evangelists in Amsterdam.*

# Chapter Eight
# Organizing for Persuasion

## *H. Eddie Fox*

D. T. Niles, the famous theologian, said that everybody needs three Christian conversions—conversion to Jesus Christ, conversion to the Christian ethic, and conversion to the Christian community. He goes on to say that people approach the faith at any one of those points. Some people are attracted to Jesus Christ, which leads them to the church, and the church leads them to express it in a Christian ethic. Other people are attracted by the Christian values and ethics of the Christian faith. Those are the people who send their children to church, wanting their children to receive those values that the parents, even though they are not Christians, still hold as important. They are attracted to the ethic, which leads them to meet Jesus, which leads them to the Christian community. Other people are attracted to the Christian community; there they meet Jesus and begin to live the life of discipleship. In our culture, people often begin with the church; they come into fellowship, and they are introduced to Jesus and begin to move toward discipleship.

If that is true, on a given Sunday there are many people on the fringes of fellowship. If those people show up at the primary worship service, the pastor is called upon to preach an evangelistic message for response in that setting.

When people come into the fringes of our fellowship, we must know who these people are in order to communicate this message effectively. The miracle of Pentecost was not the speaking. The miracle of Pentecost was the hearing. Each one heard in his or her own language—Cretans and Arabians, Medes and dwellers in Mesopotamia. If we are to preach the gospel for response, we must know who these people are in order that the gospel may be heard in their language.

John Wesley was a graduate of Oxford University. He was capable of preaching deep, intellectual messages. Yet he wrote in his diary, "I consented to be more vile." That is, he decided to speak in the common language of the ordinary people. And he instructed his preachers, as far as possible, to use one-syllable words. The common people heard and understood Wesley. If we are to preach this gospel to people who are on the edges, we need to speak a language they can understand. We must speak the language of the outsider, not the insider.

The secular world knows a great deal about persuasion, and we can learn from the secular world in the process of communication. Dr. Lawrence Lacour, professor of preaching, pastor, and evangelist, utilized secular communication theory in developing the following principles of evangelistic preaching. These steps can help us become more effective in our preaching.

## Attention

The first sentence of a sermon is vitally important, and what happens there is critical to the whole message. The only thing worse than a preacher who doesn't know how to land, is one who doesn't know how to take off. We dance around, circle, and then finally get on the runway and prepare to take off. But people won't wait very long. They change the channel; they tune us out. If we want to minister the gospel effectively, we must get their attention quickly.

# Need

Once we have their attention, we must begin with the hearers' point of need, not our own. Jesus always began at the place where the person was. He began at the point of the hearer. Evangelistic preaching has to do that. We need to begin where the people are, not where the text is. If we begin where our listeners are in their experience or journey, whatever grips those people, whatever concerns that congregation, we can ultimately demonstrate how the gospel meets that need. We begin by standing in that person's shoes, empathizing with the hearers.

Charles Wesley, the great hymn writer, wrote about six thousand hymns. Most of them were set to the music out of the pubs of his day, the popular beat and rhythm. They started where the people were. Sometimes people don't accept the treasure because the vessel is not familiar. The truth must be perceived as a part of the real world if listeners are to give us their attention.

Jesus met people where they were. His message was different for each person he encountered. He said to Nicodemus, "You've got to be born again." To the woman at the well he said, "I'll give you living water." Simon Peter needed a bigger challenge than he'd ever had. Jesus said, "Follow me, I'll give you something bigger. I'll make you a fisher of all people, everywhere." Zacchaeus was ostracized and lonely. Jesus said to him, "Come down, I'll go home with you. We'll eat together." Jesus always began at the point of the hearer, not at the point of his own message. The point of contact was from the hearer's viewpoint. We have a message, of course; there are givens, there is a core of truth, there is a center, but we do not start there. We need a point of contact, a bridge over which truth must travel. We begin at the point of need, at the point of contact from the hearer's viewpoint, if we are to preach the evangelistic message.

## Meeting the Need

Once we have made contact with the hearers' point of need, we can announce the Good News, the way Christ Jesus meets the deep needs of the human heart. We must ask the question, "Where in this sermon today is the Good News? Where is the Good News for these people?" A lot of what goes under the name of evangelism is "dis-angelism"—bad news! Often we have to listen long and hard to hear a good word from God. But I'm convinced that every message that is evangelistic must have in it good news—grace, the rule and reign of grace.

## Visualization

Preaching is visual, not linear. Jesus did not give thirty-two reasons why we should believe in the kingdom of God. He said, "The kingdom of God is like. . . . " He couched the truth in images familiar to the hearers—the pearl of great price, treasure, seeds, sowers, harvest. He was able to help his hearers visualize what the kingdom was like. That yeast is just a tiny ingredient dropped into the dough, but by the next morning it fills the whole bowl. Jesus made it clear that the kingdom is just like that. It looks so tiny, but it will fill the whole bowl. It looks small now, but one day, some day, it will fill the earth. The little mustard seed becomes a tree so big that the birds will build a nest in it. Visualization helps the hearers understand the truth and apply it in their own terms.

Visualization was the secret of Martin Luther King, Jr. Many people didn't know he was a preacher until after he died; then they played all of his sermons and discovered that the center of this man was his preaching. Martin Luther King, Jr., said, "I have a dream. I have a dream that one day, the little white boy and the little black boy are going to walk across the mountains in north Georgia, going to go across the mountains in Alabama, going to cross the hills in Mississippi." And by the time he got through, millions of people who could not give you all the reasons why the races should get together could nevertheless see the picture of what it will be like when it comes true.

That final day in Memphis, Dr. King was so tired and he didn't want to preach. The people wouldn't let him stay in his room. So he went over to preach, and he said to those people: "I've been to the mountain, I haven't been to the other side, but I've been up there and I've looked on the other side, and this is what I see." And by the time he got through, his audience said, "I see it too." He communicated, as Jesus did, with images, and the people responded to the message.

## Action

Once the need has been identified, and visualized, the last step is action. In my denomination, the invitation, the challenge to action, is the most neglected element of worship. The invitation tends to be ignored, or it tends to be the same thing every time, which is another way of ignoring it. I'm convinced that the invitation has to be a part of every gospel presentation.

Some people think the invitation was invented by the nineteenth-century camp meeting phenomenon. But it goes back a lot further than that—all the way to the Acts of the Apostles. Even C. H. Dodd in 1935 identified the appeal for repentance as a regular part of New Testament gospel presentations. Always there is a proclamation and an invitation. It's never separate. Justin Martyr, describing the worship at Rome in the early church, said the Scriptures are read, the admonitions are given, and people are invited to practice. When we talk about the invitation, we're not talking about just reviving something from the camp meeting. We're talking about being true to the gospel, the nature of the gospel, the integrity of the gospel. Proclamation leads to invitation.

The invitation comes out of the nature of the gospel. The reason we can invite people to say yes to God, is that God says yes to us first. We don't ask people to say yes to God in the hope that God will say yes. The Scripture, in 2 Corinthians 1:20, tells us that God has already said yes to us. Christ Jesus is God's yes to all of God's promises. God has already acted in Jesus Christ, and our response to him makes it possible for us to live in terms of that pardon. If we don't accept it, we're still living in bondage, but God acts first.

We evangelize because God is an evangelistic God; theology, not ecclesiology, shapes our evangelism. Some people think we're recruiting for the church. But the church is the program of evangelism, rather than the other way around. The church doesn't have a program of evangelism, the church doesn't have a mission; the church is the vehicle of God's evangelistic mission.

If the church has a program of evangelism, we can vote it in or vote it out, or put in on our bulletin this year and take it off next year. But evangelism is rooted in the nature of God. God says yes; God is an evangelistic God.

Second, the invitation is related to the purpose of the message. If we ask most preachers, "Tell me the purpose of your sermon," we get the thesis, what the sermon is about. But the purpose has to do with the response that's being sought. So the legitimate question is: What is the response being sought from the hearer as a result of preaching this message? Billy Graham is clear about the response that's being sought when he preaches that message. And in that public arena, the stadium, he understands that clear call to commitment to Jesus Christ, or that forgiveness of sins, or that being set free of bondage.

So we need to ask the question: What is my purpose? If I can't get my purpose down in a sentence, I'm probably not very clear about it. If I get that down, then I've got the makings of the invitation. If I don't have a purpose in my sermons, then I really don't have a sermon.

In addition to clarity of purpose, we need integrity. A Christian evangelist cannot use just any methodology. I once watched an evangelist giving an invitation say, "We're going to have a prayer. Everybody who wants me to pray for you, I'd like for you to just raise your hand." Some people did, but the preacher didn't pray. He said, "We're going to have a prayer. Everybody who'd like me to pray for you, those of you who raised your hand, I'd just like to ask you to stand wherever you are. We're going to have a prayer." Some people did stand, but the preacher still didn't pray. He said, "We're going to have a prayer, and I'd like to ask all of you standing to come on down here to the front."

Now, if the preacher thought it was important to ask the people to do three things, and then pray, he could have said, "We're going to do three things: I'll ask you to raise your hand; then I'll ask you to stand; then you'll come on down here, and we'll have a prayer." It would have been ill-conceived, but at least it would have been honest.

We must not cajole or manipulate people and then justify doing so by the results we get. The gospel we preach holds us under indictment, and we'll have to be accountable. And we cannot lack integrity and abuse humanity as we extend and offer this invitation.

Finally, we need to trust the Holy Spirit. God alone is in control of the response to our preaching; our responsibility is to be true to the Word of God, and to be people of integrity.

Another pastor once said to me, "I never give an invitation; it's not part of our church tradition."

"Do you offer Communion in your church?" I asked.

"Of course!" he responded.

I explained to him that when we offer Communion in our church tradition, we say, "You that do truly and earnestly repent of your sin, and are in love and charity with your neighbor, and intend to lead a new life following the commandment of God and walking henceforth in God's holy way, draw near with faith and take this holy sacrament to your comfort, making your confession to Almighty God." It's unthinkable that we would break the bread, lift the cup, and then go home without eating and drinking.

In evangelism, as in Communion, the invitation leads to response. We break the bread and lift the cup, and then give the people, by the power of the Spirit, the opportunity of responding to that invitation. We preach the word, give the invitation, and offer to people the opportunity to say yes to God in Christ Jesus.

*H. Eddie Fox is World Director of Evangelism for the World Methodist Council. He has also served for sixteen years as pastor of Methodist churches in Tennessee and Virginia, and founded the "Offering Christ Today" schools of evangelism which have attracted more than six thousand participants. He is the author of several books, including* Living a New Life, *and* Inherit the Kingdom. *This chapter is taken from his message, "Preaching for Response," delivered at the Billy Graham School of Evangelism, Buffalo, New York, August 1988.*

# Chapter Nine
# The Place of Decision

*Leighton Ford*

The average pastor today would be rather shocked if the congregation cried out at the end of his sermon, "What shall we do?" His homiletics class would not very likely have prepared him for this situation! A typical reply might be: "Well, . . . let us all consider this very carefully to see if there is anything that we would want to do now or some time in the future!"

Peter's response, when this question was raised to him at Pentecost, was to call for an immediate and definite response from his hearers: "And Peter said to them, 'Repent, and be baptized every one of you in the name of Jesus Christ for the forgiveness of your sins; and you shall receive the gift of the Holy Spirit'" (Acts 2:38, RSV).

Christian evangelistic preaching means preaching for a verdict. It is first the indicative mood: a declaration of what God has done. But it is also preaching in the imperative mood: a demand for what God commands man to do. Our Lord himself gave the example: "Jesus came into Galilee, preaching the gospel of God, and saying, 'The time is fulfilled, and the kingdom of God is at hand; repent, and believe in the gospel'" (Mark 1:14–15, RSV). Jesus constantly used the imperative. There was an urgency, an immediacy—yet with a strong note of warning to count the cost—in his appeals. "Follow me. . . believe in me . . . come after me," he said; but he also commanded, "Take up your cross . . . forsake all that you have."

"Choose! Decide!" Christ demanded. Yes or no!

"Our business," said James Black, "is serious gunfire with a target." The Lausanne Covenant describes evangelism as:

> the proclamation of the historical, biblical Christ as Savior and Lord, with a view to persuading people to come to him personally and so be reconciled to God. In issuing the Gospel invitation, we have no liberty to conceal the cost of discipleship.

## Theological Issues

Many preachers, such as the late Dr. Donald Gray Barnhouse and Dr. Martyn Lloyd-Jones, have refused to make any public invitation. They apparently have felt a theological inconsistency between the doctrines of man's inability, grace, and God's election, and such appeals. Their objection, of course, is not to spiritual decision and conversion, but rather to any method which may seem to put undue stress on the psychological aspects of decision. The whole question revolves around the issue of God's sovereignty and man's responsibility, or what God does as King and what he does as Judge.

A young man came to the Scottish preacher, John McNeil. He was on the point of graduating from theological college and was deeply concerned, as he went out to preach, for fear he might offer free grace to some who were not of the elect. "Laddie," replied Dr. McNeil with a twinkle in his eye, "don't you be worried. If you should get the wrong man saved, the Lord will forgive you for it!" McNeil's practical good humor may be of more help than all the theological wrangling that has divided Calvinists and Arminians.

But we must recognize, as J. I. Packer has said, that there is a real antinomy in Scripture—not just a paradox, but an apparent incompatibility between God's sovereignty and human free will. We cannot solve it. We must learn to live with it. And we must avoid the temptation either to an exclusive concern with human responsibility, which makes us panicky and alarmist, or to an exclusive concern with divine sovereignty, which can make us cynical about all evangelistic endeavors.[1]

There are plenty of biblical precedents for holding these two truths together. In Matthew 11:27 (RSV) Jesus said, "No one knows the Father except the Son and anyone to whom the Son chooses to reveal him," but this did not prevent our Lord from giving in the very next verse this all-inclusive invitation: "Come to me, all who labor and are heavy laden, and I will give you rest." He put the two truths in one sentence in John 6:37 (RSV): "All that the Father gives me will come to me; and him who comes to me I will not cast out." Paul's magnificent discussion of God's election in Romans 9 did not prevent him from having a great burden and yearning of heart. Indeed, he opens that very chapter with these words:

> I am speaking the truth in Christ, I am not lying; my conscience bears me witness in the Holy Spirit, that I have great sorrow and unceasing anguish in my heart. For I could wish that I myself were accursed and cut off from Christ for the sake of my brethren, my kinsmen by race" (Romans 9:1–3, RSV).

If we feel that we cannot give an invitation for a sinner to come to Christ, because of man's inability, we need to remember that Jesus invited a man whose hand was paralyzed to do what he could not do. "Stretch out your hand," Jesus commanded (Matthew 12:13), and the man obeyed the command and did what he could not do. Jesus also told the dead man to do something he could not do—live! "Lazarus, come forth," he commanded (John 11:43), and Lazarus obeyed the voice of Jesus and did what he could not do.

A friend of mine was discussing evangelism with a professor of theology. The professor, who places a strong emphasis on the sacraments, was objecting strenuously to evangelistic

---

[1]J. I. Packer, *Evangelism and the Sovereignty of God* (Downers Grove, Ill.: InterVarsity Press, 1961), 18-36.

appeals as used in modern campaigns. He maintained that we must preach the gospel and leave the matter there. My friend replied, "Professor, you are always emphasizing to us the importance of the sacraments in the Christian life. Now, is it enough to display the wine and the bread on the Communion table, and to declare objectively that this stands for our Lord's broken body and poured-out blood? Of course it is not. We must also go on to give the invitation in Christ's place, 'Take, eat. Take, drink.' And this," my friend went on, "is what the evangelist is doing when he says, 'Come to Jesus.'"

We must beware of making our evangelistic appeal all imperative and no indicative, or else of so dividing between the indicative and the imperative that we give people the impression that God is responsible for 50 percent of our salvation and we for the other 50 percent. Salvation is "all of grace." "We must beware of making a Christ out of our faith," declared Spurgeon. "The trembling hand can receive a golden gift." We are saved "by grace, through faith." It is grace that saves; it is faith that receives. And even that faith is "not from yourselves, it is the gift of God" (Ephesians 2:8). God commands all people everywhere to repent and believe, but even in our decision, God does not leave us on our own. His grace is offered in his command, and his grace works in our response.

Faith in God's sovereign grace and salvation has helped me in two basic attitudes toward my evangelistic work. First, it has kept me from losing heart, from pessimism. Only the sovereignty of God is sufficient ground for preaching for a verdict. Otherwise, evangelism is a hopeless task. We are told in Scripture that the "natural man does not accept the things of the Spirit of God" (1 Corinthians 2:14, NASB). We learn that "the carnal mind . . . is not subject to the law of God, neither indeed can be" (Romans 8:7, KJV). Outside of Christ, men are dead in trespasses and sins (Ephesians 2:1) and blinded by the god of this world (2 Corinthians 4:4). How can a dead man live and a blind man see? With God, all things are possible.

Ananias must have felt that Saul was a hopeless case, when the word came to him that he should go to this arch-persecutor of the church and lay his hands on him. Ananias protested,

"Lord, I have heard from many about this man, how much evil he has done to thy saints at Jerusalem" (Acts 9:13, RSV). But the Lord said to him, "Go, for he is a chosen instrument of mine" (v. 15, RSV). Ananias said, in effect, "See how much evil he has done—it is impossible that he be converted." But God said, "He is a chosen vessel—nothing is impossible with me."

This confidence in God also guards us from self-dependence, from opportunism. There is a great danger in the success/status psychology of our day. The pressure to produce results lies particularly heavy on the evangelist. The pastor is also pushed to "get results" in our competitive society—more members, better programs, and bigger attendance. This pressure leads to trusting in techniques and manipulation, and brings the danger of leading people into premature, abortive decisions before they have really faced up to the meaning of the gospel and the demands of the Christian life. The last state of such a person is often worse than the first.

God holds me responsible for "faithful evangelism," not for success. Therefore, I may plead, but never coerce. Our pattern is Jesus, who never manipulated or forced people. When the rich young ruler came in his eagerness and went away sad, Jesus watched his retreating figure with an unutterable grief. But he did not run after him. He did not strong-arm his way into his life. He neither lowered his demands nor increased the pressure.

So must we, when we invite men to Christ, keep very close to the scriptural pattern and the biblical terminology, and invite men to come to God in the name of Christ who is not a beggar but imperial Lord.

## Emotional Issues

Many people react against all appeals because they have been put off by experiences of invitations which have been given without taste, without tact, without dignity, and with a questionable emotional manipulation of people.

I think we must learn to distinguish between emotionalism and emotion. Emotionalism is emotion isolated, emotion for emotion's sake. There is a legitimate place for emotion in preaching the gospel. Nothing truly human lacks emotion. When we think back to experiences that have left their imprint on us, there will certainly have been some deep and great emotion connected with the experience. In this whole matter of emotions we have tended to one of two extremes: to be overzealous or overcautious. By and large, the orthodox churches have been far too restrained. That is why many of the sect groups are growing so rapidly. As Dr. John Mackay says, "Something is wrong when emotion becomes legitimate in everything except religion."

A Tennessee mountain preacher put emotion in the right perspective. "Today we go to the football game to do our shouting," he says, "to the movies to do our crying, and to church to do our freezing!" And he provided a good test of the reality of the emotional aspect of any experience when he said, "I don't care how high you jump, or how loud you shout, as long as when you hit the ground you walk straight!"

But we must recognize clearly the real danger involved in a decision that is primarily emotional. It is usually followed by a pendulum-like backward swing when hard realities challenge the emotional assurance. And this results either in a constant attempt to reproduce the emotional state, thus in an unbalanced Christian life; or in a feeling of betrayal and suspicion, and reaction against any religious experience at all.

As evangelists, we should remember that we are speaking to the whole person—intellect, conscience, emotion, will—and that God wants the response of the whole person. "Thou shalt love the Lord thy God with all thy heart, and with all thy soul, and with all thy mind, and with all thy strength" (Mark 12:30, KJV).

There should be an appeal to the intellect, a strong emphasis on teaching, in an evangelistic ministry. "Obey the truth"— that is how Paul described the response to the gospel. Luke described Paul's ministry, saying he "disputed" (Acts 9:29), or "reasoned" (Acts 17:2), or "taught" (Acts 18:11), or "persuaded" (Acts 18:4). But the evangelist also speaks to the conscience, as Paul said in 2 Corinthians 4:2: "We commend ourselves to every man's conscience." There is a type of evangelistic message which is 10 percent teaching and 90 percent appeal. This reverses the proportion of the New Testament. Through the avenues of intellect, conscience, and emotion, we seek to reach the central citadel where a person will in the total personality say yes to the yes of God in Christ.

I am convinced that giving some kind of public invitation to come to Christ is not only theologically correct, but also emotionally sound. People need this opportunity for expression. The inner decision for Christ is like driving a nail through a board. The open declaration of it is like clinching the nail on the other side, so that it is not easily pulled out. Impression without expression can lead to depression. William James said, "When once the judgment is decided let a man commit himself; let him lay on himself the necessity of doing more, let him lay on himself the necessity of doing all. Let him take a public pledge if the case allows. Let him envelop his resolution with all the aids possible."

To be sure, there are emotional dangers involved. People can respond to a hypercharged atmosphere, or to some pathetic story. We must be careful that in the evangelistic presentation, everything is planned and carried out so that the truth of the Word of God stands central and supreme, and is the focus of attention. We must also be sure to warn people that the Christian life does not move on moods and thrills, but by trust and obedience. The initial moment of decision is a needed and helpful highlight, but it is no more the whole of the Christian life than the honeymoon is the whole of marriage. We must also warn people not to confuse emotional experience with spiritual reality. Our Lord spoke of the seed which sprang up quickly but had no root, and compared it to those who receive a sermon with joy but soon fade away. And we must remember that some neurotic or disturbed individuals usually respond to all such appeals; they need sensitive and expert counseling.

Yet, having recognized the pitfalls, I am still persuaded that the blessings of direct evangelism, which confronts people to a point of decision, far outweigh the perils.

## Practical Issues

The dual danger of the invitation lies either in having no method of bringing people to Christ, or else idolizing one method. We must beware of imagining that we can put the Holy Spirit in a box and dictate how everyone must come to Christ. Many seeking and believing souls have been frustrated for years because they have been unable to reproduce exactly the experience of conversion a friend went through.

A leading Baptist churchman once said that when he was converted at a camp meeting in his youth, he went forward and knelt at an old-fashioned altar. Someone came along and clapped him on one shoulder, saying, "Brother, come and hold on." Another person hit him on the other shoulder and said, "Brother, come and let go!" The third man said, "When I was saved, a big light came from heaven and hit me right in the face." "Between holding on, and letting go, and looking for the light," the preacher said, "I almost missed the kingdom of God!"

Jesus healed many blind men during his ministry. And he healed each of them in a unique way. To one man, he simply said, "Receive your sight," and the man saw. But for another man he mixed mud and put it on his eyes, and told him to go and wash it off. Now suppose those two men had met years later. One might have inquired of the other, "What did Jesus do for you?"

"I was blind and Jesus made me see."

"You don't say! Jesus gave me back my sight, too. How did he heal you?"

The second man would say, "He simply said for me to see, and my eyesight came."

"He didn't put mud on your eyes? He didn't send you down to the river to wash it off? Why, man, you can't see at all! You're still blind!"

And if they had been like our modern churches, they would have made two different denominations out of it: the "Muddites" and the "Anti-Muddites!"

## Methods of Invitation

No one method is suitable for every Sunday, every church, and every culture. I have preached in conservative churches or areas where people are very reserved, and have not felt it wise to ask people to come forward, particularly in a smaller meeting, but rather have asked them to remain after the service or come to another room for counseling. On the other hand, we have been in areas of the world where people are very free and unrestrained in the expression of their feelings, and everyone would flood forward in open public invitation. In that situation, we have also asked people to remain behind and to seek counseling after the service. The truth is that some method or other is right everywhere. There are many approaches in inviting people to decision.

(a) *The invitation to come forward at the close of a sermon.* The advantage of this method is that it is clear-cut and decisive. The disadvantage is that some will hold back because of shyness, or rebel because they regard it as an unseemly form of exhibitionism. After experimenting with many different approaches in many different situations, I have become convinced that in most instances the following approach is the best.

When a minister expects to give this invitation, it is wise to explain ahead of time, before or during his sermon, what he intends to do, and then build toward this moment of decision throughout the entire message. The invitation should not be tacked on at the end as an afterthought. Neither should it be anti-climactic. It is a mistake for the preacher to build to a great height, closing with some powerful story, and then almost visibly let down as he says, "Now we invite you to come to Christ." The evangelistic sermon ought to move on a constantly ascending line as it comes to its climax, and a high moment ought to come when the preacher finishes his appeal and says, "Now come."

If you are going to give an invitation, prepare your invitation as you do the rest of your sermon. Think through clearly what you are going to say and do. Plan with the choir and the choir director your final hymn, and who will sing it, and whether or not you will pause after certain verses. Have a definite place prepared for counseling with those who come forward, whether in front of the sanctuary or auditorium, or in another room.

When you give the appeal, explain the reason you give it. Remember that the procedure is unfamiliar to many people. Explain it as a means of obeying Christ's command to confess him before men, and a step which will help to make the decision definite and clear-cut. Make the invitation as straightforward as possible. Avoid vague appeals which imply that everyone should come. If your object is to reach people who are making a first-time commitment to Christ, say so. If you are also including those who are coming back to Christ, or those who may want to come for assurance, say so.

I have found it helpful to speak of the symbolism involved in the invitation. It is an open sign of an inward decision. A man makes a promise, says in his heart *I'll keep my word*, and shakes hands as a sign. A soldier sees the flag go by. In his heart, he says, *I'll be loyal to my country.* He salutes—it is a sign. A young couple commit themselves to each other in their hearts and pledge their loyalty in the giving of self. Then they stand at the front of the church and pledge themselves openly—in word, by the giving of rings, and by the sign of a kiss. It is a visible sign of their inward commitment. So when people come from their seats and stand at the front, it is an open sign that, as they come physically to the front, so they are coming with their hearts to Jesus Christ.

We must, by all means, avoid deception. There is danger in asking people to go through several steps; first to raise their hand, then to stand, then to come forward. Some people will raise a hand who would have no intention of going forward, and if they did so would later feel that they had been tricked and betrayed. It is far better to explain clearly and ask people to take just one step. It is also important to tell people what will happen to them after they come forward, especially for the sake of strangers and those who are not familiar with invitations.

I have known of people who have been afraid to come forward to "confess Christ" because they think this means they will go into a counseling room and have to confess their sins publicly. When you give the appeal, say, "After you have come forward, we would like to have a prayer with you and give you a further word of instruction about the Christian life, to have some counseling with you and to answer your questions, to give you some literature which will help you to read your Bible and to go on in the Christian life, and then you may go or rejoin your friends." What will happen should be clearly explained before, not after people have come forward.

(b) *The "after-service."* In some cases, it may be wise to ask those who want to make their decision or inquire further about Christian commitment to remain behind, or go to another room after the main service. The advantage of this is that it gives people time to think and reaches some shy people who could never bring themselves to come forward. The disadvantage is that it is not quite as decisive and allows an "out" to some who might have come forward. But, after all, our trust is not in the method but in the Lord. He who convicts the heart in the first place is surely able to bring people to himself in this way.

The pattern for an after-service varies widely, but it is a method which has been used successfully for many years. Evangelists such as D. L. Moody and Dr. R. A. Torrey made much more use of an after-service than of the invitation to come forward.

In leading up to an after-service, the evangelist might say something like this: "At the end of the sermon tonight, I am going to lead in a brief prayer. Following the prayer, there will be an opportunity for those of you who wish to leave, or must leave, to do so. Then we are going to have a brief after-meeting for all of you who can remain, in which I am going to state as clearly as I know how the steps in coming to Jesus Christ. I hope that all of you who can will stay. If you are not a Christian and you wish to become a Christian, please stay. If you are not sure and you wish to make sure, I invite you to stay. If you are not prepared yet to come to Christ, but you want to know more about it, you are welcome to stay. If you are already committed to Christ, I hope that you will stay to encourage others. The fact that you stay does not mean that you are not a Christian. The fact that you go, if you wish to or must, does not mean that you are not interested. If you do stay, no one will approach you or embarrass you in any way. The after-service will not last more than ten minutes."

Dismiss with a brief prayer, ask the organist or pianist to play quietly, and give an opportunity for those who are leaving to do so quickly and quietly. Ask the ushers then to close the doors. If the remaining crowd is scattered, you may wish to ask them all to come toward the front, and to go down and speak to them from the floor of the church or auditorium.

At this point I have usually asked people to bow in a moment of silent prayer, asking God to speak to them. I then give as clearly and as concisely as possible the steps in becoming a Christian (as outlined below). Often I have asked those who wish to make this decision to repeat silently after me a prayer of commitment, and then to raise their hands as a sign if they have made a decision. I then explain the importance of confessing Christ openly, and ask those who have made the decision and have so indicated to come and tell me of their decision at the close of the after-service; to take a card which they will sign as an affirmation of their faith; and to receive some literature and, if possible, personal counseling. Then the after-service is dismissed with a benediction. It is most important that the after-service be promptly concluded within the time limits announced.

(c) *Instruction in the counseling room or after-service.* Whether you are speaking to inquirers who have come forward at an invitation, or to people who have remained behind for an after-service, it is important to put them at ease by a warm but reverent attitude. I believe this is especially important when inquirers have been taken to another room, for many are wondering what will be done to them. It may be wise to say, "We welcome you in the name of Christ. Perhaps you are wondering just what we are going to do to you, and how you will ever get out of here, if you get out! Well, I want to assure you that we are not going to do anything to you, or put you through the 'third degree.' You are not going to be embarrassed, and you don't have to make a speech. We wanted to have this chance to share something more of the meaning of the Christian life, to have a prayer of commitment together, and to help you in going on with Christ."

At this point, some clear explanation needs to be made of how to come to Christ. While we want to avoid hackneyed expressions and stereotyped formulas, I have felt it vital to present these basic truths in an easily remembered fashion. The gospel may be presented in terms of the *Three R's*—in coming to Christ we must *recognize* our need, be prepared to *renounce* our sin, and to *receive* Christ. Or we may speak of the *ABCD's*: There is something to *admit*—that I have sinned, that I cannot save myself, that I need a Savior; there is something to *believe*—that Jesus Christ is the Savior and that he is able and willing to save me; there is something to *consider*—the cost of becoming a Christian, that Jesus is not only to be Savior but also my Lord; and there is something to *do*—I am not only to believe about Christ, but I am to entrust myself to him. In terms of Revelation 3:20, I not only believe that he wants to come in, but open the door of my life and I ask him in.

Mark 1:14–17 (RSV) gives an excellent summary of Christian decision:

> Jesus came into Galilee, preaching the gospel of God, and saying, "The time is fulfilled, and the kingdom of God is at hand; repent, and believe in the gospel." And passing along by the Sea of Galilee, he saw Simon and Andrew the brother of Simon casting a net in the sea; for they were fishermen. And Jesus said to them, "Follow me and I will make you become fishers of men."

First of all Jesus declared something that God had done, and then he demanded something that men must do. This demand is found in three imperatives: (1) repent, (2) believe the gospel, (3) follow me.

To repent not only means that I acknowledge I have sinned, not only that I am sorry about it, but that I change my mind about sin, about God, and about myself—I am ready for God to change my life; I am ready to leave my sin. To believe the gospel not only means to give mental assent, but to give commitment of the will. I may believe there is a glass of water and know that

I am thirsty, but the water will not help me unless I drink it. And Jesus calls us, knowing that when we do believe, the result will be a life of service. "Follow me," he says.

This explanation of becoming a Christian may also be considered in terms of the great biblical word "Come." This is especially appropriate when people have come forward out of a crowd to the front, as a symbol of their coming to Jesus Christ. How do we come to Christ? We come humbly, knowing that we have sinned.

The only person for whom Jesus can do nothing is a man who thinks he is so good that he needs nothing. The three hardest words in the English language to say, and really mean, are, "I have sinned." But when I come to Jesus I come humbly, knowing my sin and being willing to turn from it. When I come to Jesus, I come in faith.

How do I know that if I come he will receive me? I know because of the Cross. There God says that he has taken care of my sin, that Christ has borne it for me. And God's promise, no matter what I have done or been, is that it is all right to come home. He wants me to come. When I come to Christ, I come in surrender. I am not only asking him to forgive my past, and someday to take me to heaven, but I am coming to follow him here and now. He came to save me not only *from* my sins but *for* his service. I am deciding not merely to make one decision, but to enter into a life of decision in which I will daily come to Jesus Christ as my Lord.

Such explanation leads naturally into a prayer of commitment. For practical reasons, in large crusades we often do this as a group prayer with all those who have come forward. But I much prefer to have the inquirer pray personally, in the company of some trained and qualified counselor. This makes it possible for the prayer to be much more personal, and more in line with particular needs and the specific decisions about them which that person is making. Sometimes, when a small group has come to an after-service or to a counseling room in a church, after explaining the way to Christ, I have asked each member of the group to pray just one sentence out loud, according to their particular decision, whether it be rededication, assurance, or first-time commitment—even suggesting a sentence that they might pray, such as "Lord Jesus, come into my heart," or "I thank you for dying for me," or "I want you to be Lord of all. I dedicate my life to you."

Whether in a group or individually, the inquirer is sometimes shy and needs some guidance as to what to pray. So it is often helpful to lead in a prayer and ask the inquirer(s) to repeat the prayer out loud phrase by phrase. The prayer should be quite simple and direct: "Oh God, I come to you today, as best I know how. I come to you humbly, for I know that I have sinned, and I want to turn from my sin. I come to you in faith, for I believe Christ loved me and died for me. I do trust him now as my Savior. Come into my heart, Lord Jesus. I come to you in surrender. Take my life and help me to follow you, in your church, and in my daily life. I thank you for receiving me. In Jesus' name. Amen."

Two points are very important to stress with any inquirer. One is the matter of *assurance*. We need to distinguish between the sense of relief, which may be based on temporary emotion, and permanent assurance which is based on conviction brought by the Holy Spirit from the never-changing Word of God. Often in speaking to those who have "made a decision," I ask if they know now that they belong to Christ and that he is in their heart. Sometimes the answer comes, "Oh yes. I feel so clean. I feel as if a burden has been lifted. I feel a great joy." We ought not to criticize or belittle such feelings. Emotional experiences are a genuine part of coming to Christ, and there is joy and peace in believing. What we need to do is to point out that such feelings do not always come immediately to the new convert, and they certainly do not always last. There will come times of pressure, of doubt, and of temptation, when converts will question the reality of their relationship with Christ. Then they need to have far more than a feeling on which to base their faith.

I often take a simple verse of Scripture, such as John 1:12, or John 6:37, or Revelation 3:20, and ask inquirers to read that verse carefully. I then ask if they have fulfilled the condition— if they have received Christ, or come to him, or opened the door to him. If the answer is yes, I then go on to ask if they now are the child of God, if Christ has received them, if he has come into their heart. Very often the answer will be, "Well, I think so," or "I hope so."

I then hold out a New Testament, or a pencil, and say, "If I told you I was going to give this to you tomorrow, and you went home and told someone that you were going to get a gift tomorrow, and they asked how you knew, what would you reply?" The obvious answer is, "Leighton Ford told me."

"How can you be sure of it?"

"Because I can trust you."

"Well, can you trust God? Has he told you that he will receive you, save you, come into your life? And has he done it? How do you know? Because God says so."

This point needs to be made again and again, until the inquirers see—and often it will burst in with a glorious light upon their souls—that their relationship with Christ does not depend on what they have done, and on what they feel. It depends on what he has done, and on what he says.

Great discernment is necessary at this point, of course. We do not want to give false assurance to the person who is resisting the Holy Spirit and who is holding back from receiving Christ. We must not seek to bring assurance prematurely, before the issues of salvation by grace through faith, of repentance from sin, of commitment to discipleship have been faced. But to honest souls who have sincerely accepted Christ, we can point to this assurance and pray that the Holy Spirit will witness in their hearts to the truth of the Word.

We need equally to stress that the decision for Christ is only the beginning. It is a beginning of a pilgrimage, not an end. It is like the gun that starts a race. Like a newborn baby, the inquirer needs spiritual food in order that he may grow. The importance of Bible reading, of daily prayer, of fellowship and service in the church, of sharing Christ with others by the witness of life and conversation, should be underlined—not as arbitrary rules, but as the means of letting Jesus Christ pour his life into ours, and through ours to others. The Christian life may be pictured as a wheel, with Christ as the hub at the center, and the rim being the Christian coming into contact with the world about him. The spokes of the wheel—the Word of God, prayer, witnessing, obedience, fellowship—are the means by which the power of Christ keeps the Christian moving.

(*d*) *Other methods of invitation.* A wide variety of methods have been used by different pastors and evangelists. Tom Rees, the British lay evangelist, closes his meetings with an "act of witness," as he calls it, and asks all those who have received Christ in the last two years to take part in it. This provides a helpful opportunity for public witness to many who have privately or in some other service committed their lives to Christ.

Dr. Ronald Ward, the Anglican evangelist, has a card placed in the pews in a church where he is conducting a mission. On this card is printed a statement of acceptance of Christ or of dedication of life. During a period of meditation at the close of his sermon, he will ask the congregation to take up the card and request those who are prepared to make their decision to fill it in and then take it with them after the benediction to another room, where they have a period of counseling.

We have used a variation on this in some of our crusades, distributing to everyone at the beginning of the service a card which requests further information on how to become a Christian, or how to have assurance of salvation. We then ask those who have not come forward at the conclusion of the service, but would like more information, to fill in the card and leave it in a box at the door, or send it in to our office by mail. A helpful booklet is then sent to them, and if possible a counselor calls on them personally at their home to speak with them further.

Alan Walker, the Australian Methodist, has found it helpful during his invitation at his Sunday evening theater services in Sydney, to have certain specified counselors walk to the front of their aisle during each verse of the hymn of invitation, and then to guide those who come forward during the singing of that verse to the counseling room. Some churches will ask elders or deacons to come and stand at the front during the invitation, as a means of encouraging those who wish to make their decision.

An interesting letter from Conrad Thompson, a Lutheran secretary of evangelism, describes the methods which some Lutherans are using in their missions. He encourages the pastors to spend some time on one of the evenings explaining the various types of decisions to which the Holy Spirit leads people—both Christians and non-Christians.

Then an invitation is given for anyone who would like to come to the altar and kneel and meet God privately there. Hundreds of Lutheran churches, he reports, have done this. Thousands of their people have gone to kneel and to rededicate their lives to Christ, or to give their hearts to him at that time.

An even more popular consecration service is the reiteration of the confirmation vows. In this they ask the same questions that they do in the confirmation service, except that the people are asked to answer in silence. At the conclusion of the questions the leader says, "There is one part of the service which was purposely left out—the part which says, 'Give me your hand in token thereof.' Tonight, we are going to ask all of you to leave by way of the center aisle through one door, and all of you shake hands with your pastor. Some of you may be led by God to place your hand in the hand of your pastor and say, 'I will,' as evidence of your commitment to Jesus Christ tonight."

Many Lutheran pastors, Thompson claims, have said that this has been the high point in their entire ministry. He also describes a number of other ideas used, such as the testimony meeting, the Communion service, and the confession of sin and private absolution service from the liturgy as people come to the altar and kneel. He concludes, "I do not want to give the impression that this is a mass movement in the Lutheran Church, but it has been multiplied tremendously in the last several years."

Among young people, the "say-so" meeting and the "fireside service" have been very helpful. The former is exactly what it implies—an informal meeting at the end of a conference or week of services, during which young people who have made some commitment to Jesus Christ are asked to say so—to share briefly and concisely before the group what Christ has come to mean to them. The "fireside service" takes place around a fire, and those who have made a decision for Christ are asked to come and take a stick from a pile and place it on the fire as a symbol that their lives are being given to Christ as fuel for his fire in the world. They may also be asked to express briefly the meaning of their decision.

(e) *The "guest service."* Some congregations, because of their size, location, or tradition, find it effective to give some kind of invitation at almost every service. But in many churches, an invitation given at every service loses its spontaneity, expectancy, and effectiveness, and becomes just an ineffectual—sometimes even boring—ritual. Still other churches, because of their background and tradition, would not feel comfortable with an invitation given at every service.

In such a situation a "guest service" may provide the answer. The custom has been followed particularly in many of the evangelical Anglican churches in England and Australia. One Sunday morning or evening a month is set aside as a "guest service," and the whole congregation knows when it will be held. It may also be widely advertised in the community. At this particular service, the minister will give a clear-cut evangelistic address aimed at bringing people to Christian decision. Christian people will bring to this service their friends and neighbors whom they are seeking to win for Christ and his church. At the conclusion of the sermon an invitation will be given, or an after-service held as described above.

## The Overtones of the Invitation

The inner attitude of the evangelist or pastor, and the expression of it in the manner of giving the invitation are crucial. I personally have found it very helpful to study Billy Graham, for God has given him a unique gift in calling people to Christ. This is not merely the combination of his dynamic personality and excellent preaching, and most certainly cannot be explained as crowd psychology. I am convinced rather that it grows from the inner yearning of his heart.

Joe Blinco, a former member of the Billy Graham team, tells how he was preaching in Adelaide, Australia, when Mr. Graham came in and sat at the rear of the auditorium (for he was to preach the following night). At the conclusion of the service, he came to Mr. Blinco and said, "Joe, that was a wonderful sermon. And you know at the end when you gave the invitation, I felt something welling up inside me. I wanted to stand up and ask people to come to Christ." How many of us would have felt the same yearning, if we had not been preaching a sermon?

If God leads you to give an invitation, give it with conviction—a conviction that God is calling you to do this, that you are not doing it just to conform to what people expect. Give it with courage. Be prepared to risk embarrassing failure. Even if no one responds to the invitation, it is good to give it because it emphasizes the decisiveness which is involved in following Christ.

Issue the challenge with compassion, humility, and gentleness. We are not inviting people to Christ out of a superiority complex, but because we know the life-changing power of Jesus' love. William Temple said:

> It is quite futile saying to people: "Go to the Cross." We must be able to say: "Come to the Cross." And there are only two voices which can issue that invitation with effect. One is the voice of the sinless Redeemer, with which we cannot speak; and one is the voice of the forgiven sinner, who knows himself forgiven. That is our part.[2]

Give the invitation with urgency and definiteness. Don't be wishy-washy. The invitation should not be, "If there is anyone here who might want to come, you could come, or you could wait and see me afterward." Let it rather be: "God is calling. Come now. Come here." Give it with expectancy. "According to your faith, be it unto you," said Jesus. If we do not believe anything is going to happen, it will not.

---

[2]William Temple, *Towards the Conversion of England* (London: The Press and Publications Board of the Church Assembly, 1945), 66.

Give it with absolute integrity. Make the implications clear-cut. Don't be guilty of saying, "We shall sing only one more verse," and then singing fifteen more.

Give it with empathy. Take up the desires, the fears, the questions, the hesitations and longings, of those who are deciding. Take time between some of the verses to express some of their questions, and to give brief answers to them. Do this with simplicity and straightforwardness. Don't confuse people with a multitude of instructions as to why and how they should come. Make your explanations as concise as you can.

In this matter of the invitation, there remains much room for deep thinking and wide experimentation in the church today. Dr. Helmut Thielicke, famed German preacher and theologian, sent a moving letter to Billy Graham after he had attended the crusade in Los Angeles:

> I saw them all coming towards us, I saw there their assembled, moved, and honestly decided faces, I saw their searching and meditativeness. I confess that this moved me to the very limits. Above all there were two young men—one white and one black— who stood at the front, and about whom one felt that they were standing at that moment on Mount Horeb and looking from afar into a land that they had longed for. I shall never forget those faces. It became lightning clear that men want to make a decision, and that the meditative conversation which we have cultivated in Germany since the war is only a poor fragment. I shall have to draw from all this certain consequences in my own preaching, even though the outward form will, of course, look somewhat different.

A British theological student was once sent by a professor to hear a noted preacher on the weekend. He came back with the sophisticated disgust that theological students sometimes affect, and said, "Why, that man didn't do anything but say, 'Come to Jesus'!"

"And did they come?" his professor gently asked.

"Well, yes, they did," came his grudging reply.

"I want you to go back," said the professor, "and listen to that man preach again and again, until you can say, 'Come to Jesus' as he did, and people come."

*Leighton Ford, evangelist and longtime associate of Billy Graham, is founder and president of Leighton Ford Ministries. This chapter is taken from his book,* The Christian Persuader, *published by World Wide Publications.*

# Chapter Ten
# Enthusiasm or Evangelism?

*Joe Hale*

When I was in seminary, some of my friends were talking about a young man who was "really evangelistic": he had an animated style and was a dynamic and forceful speaker. Evangelism, however, cannot be equated with these qualities; enthusiasm can easily be mistaken for evangelism. Sermons are not evangelistic because they are preached by an energetic preacher, in a series of evangelistic meetings, identified by a sign out front that bears the words, "Revival" or "Crusade."

## The Content of Evangelism

Sermons are evangelistic for two reasons: First, because they clearly set forth the gospel, which offers a new relationship with God and a changed life. Some sermons help people grow in grace, others call for our participation in the world mission of the church, and still others address wrongs that need to be challenged. Evangelistic sermons offer a new relationship with God and a changed life.

## Logic and Evangelism

Second, sermons are evangelistic because they call for response. The invitation to respond is not an afterthought that is tacked on, but a logical extension of the message itself. Most of us have attended worship services where a meaningful sermon was preached, and an invitation was given, but the invitation was not related to the sermon. The sermon was outstanding, but the invitation that followed was not "logical." When I was growing up, one minister I remember would preach his sermon, then while folding his notes and closing his Bible, he would say, "If you wish to respond to the invitation to Christian discipleship, the doors of the church are always open." It was a rote invitation, and it had little bearing or relationship to what he had been previously saying.

Sermons that are truly evangelistic are different. They call for response because an invitation for persons to put their trust in Christ naturally emerges from the sermon. If I choose a text that has evangelistic potential, the invitation will be logical. It will flow from the message, because it is intrinsic to it.

Fred Craddock, one of the great teachers of preaching today, says that we ought to be able to write in one affirmative sentence, "This is what I will say in my sermon." If it is an evangelistic sermon, we ought to be prepared to write an equally clear statement of what we hope the response will be. If we do that, we sharpen our message and make it vital and relevant to the hearers, who are asking how the sermon can possibly have any meaning for them.

## The Great Themes of Evangelism

John Wesley preached on texts that placed the burden for response on those who listened:

> I preached in the marketplace to most inhabitants of the town on "one thing is needful" (Luke 10). I believe the word carried conviction with the hearts of nearly all who heard. . . . I enforced on an

artless, loving congregation, "If any man thirst, let him come to me and drink."

They flocked from every side in a meadow near the town, and I cried aloud, "all things are ready, come." And in the afternoon at six, I preached, "Seek ye the Lord while he may be found, call upon him while he is near." I used great plainness of speech toward them.

I spoke strongly at Canterbury to the soldiers in particular, "He that hath the Son hath life, and he that hath not the Son hath not life."

Wesley continued in his journal:

I enforced on them the text, "What shall it profit a man if he gain the whole world and lose his own soul?" I cried with a loud voice, "Believe on the Lord Jesus Christ and thou shalt be saved."

He preached often from texts like: "If any man be in Christ he is a new creature," or "It is appointed upon men once to die, and after that the judgment."

Wesley usually recorded some revealing phrase about the occasion in addition to the chapter and verse: When he preached "God is a Spirit, and they that worship him must worship him in Spirit and in truth," he wrote "I applied it with all possible plainness." He was earnest, and his hearers felt it. The texts contained the evangel, which itself called for response.

Such passages leap from almost every page of both the Old and New Testaments. The call is built into their fabric. The texts John Wesley so often used in Bristol, London, and in the open air across England, called for men and women to respond to God.

Wesley's contemporary and colleague, George Whitefield, was known everywhere because over and again he preached on *two* subjects: the new birth, and justification by faith. These themes were central to the Methodist awakening in England two hundred and fifty years ago.

In 1741, Whitefield preached a series of services in Glasgow, Scotland. He spoke on "The Lord Our Righteousness" from Jeremiah 33, "The Prodigal Son" from Luke 15, "The Method of Grace" from Jeremiah 6, and "Saul's Conversion" from Acts 7.

Dwight L. Moody was the greatest evangelist of the last century. As a boy he worked as a shoe salesman in Boston, and it was while he was employed in the shoe store, a concerned man led him to faith in Jesus Christ. Soon after that, Moody moved to Chicago and began his evangelistic work as a Sunday school teacher. Moody said:

> When I began, I couldn't speak more than five minutes, so I would get up for five minutes and sit down. By and by, I got so that I could speak for fifteen minutes. If anyone were to ask me, "When did you begin to preach?" I couldn't tell him. I began with the children. By and by, they brought their parents. Then I noticed about half of the audience was adults.

Moody spoke on *themes*, rather than single texts. We can see the potential for evangelism in one of Moody's favorites, "The Love of God." You may know the story of his friendship with young Henry Moorehouse. He casually met him in Dublin, on his first visit to Great Britain. Later Moorehouse came to Chicago while Moody was away, and he asked to preach in Moody's church. Although he had met Moody in England, the officials were reluctant to let him preach in Moody's Chicago pulpit. Finally they gave in, and he spoke on John 3:16 the first night. They asked him to speak again, and the second night he spoke once again on John 3:16. By the third night Moody had returned home and went to see how this fellow was doing. The preacher got up and announced, "My text tonight is John 3:16," and again quoted it. To the amazement of all, he spoke every night for a full week on the same text. What Moorehouse did transformed Moody's ministry! Moody said, "I never knew up to that time that God loved us so much."

The love of God, the blood of Christ, prayer, faith, promises—these became Moody's themes, and they are filled with limitless possibilities in drawing people into a saving relationship with God. His thematic sermons on assurance, the Holy Ghost, what Christ is to us, grace, believing, walking with God, all opened a door to faith and invited "whosoever would" to walk through it.

## Meeting People's Needs

From the Word that is preached, the Holy Spirit moves "beyond the sacred page" toward the needs people have. We need salvation, but we can't earn it. It is a gift. God does not place a ladder in front of us and say, "Climb it, and if you reach high enough I'll accept you and love you." There is a ladder, but it is a ladder God *descends* to meet us at the point of our need.

The *evangel* is the grace of our Lord Jesus Christ that brings forgiveness. Many people long to be set free from the burden of guilt, but somehow they have not had the opportunity or have not availed themselves of moments when that release could have been theirs. People also want the assurance that "God's spirit bears witness with our spirit, that we are the children of God." These select themes are not the whole of the gospel of Jesus Christ, but they *do* have the potential for preaching that will move people toward God.

When Jesus came preaching, his first sermon was "Repent ye, for the kingdom of God is at hand." He said to the disciples, "Follow me."

"Where do you live?" they asked.

And he responded, "Come and see."

Jesus' words to people stimulated them to respond. His preaching also raised questions: "Come unto me all you that labor and are heavy laden and I will give you rest." The question is, "Have I come?" "Have I found that rest?"

At the grave of Lazarus, Jesus said, "He that believeth on me, though he were dead, yet shall he live." Then he asked, "Believest thou this?" It was the invitation to faith.

H. Grady Davis, in *Design for Preaching*, says there are five questions people in a congregation ask every time they hear a preacher:

1. "What's he talking about?"

2. "What is he saying about it?"

3. "What does he mean?"

4. "Is it true? Do I believe it?"

People will often go with us this far; but the most important question still remains:

5. "So what?"

I can know what is being said and what is meant and in general agree with it, but if I don't see it as relevant to my life, it means nothing!

When we have been touched by a sermon, in looking back we will probably see that it answered the "So what?" question. "That is where I am. It applies to me!" A sermon which answers the "So what?" question is likely to open the hearers to significant decision.


# Facing Problems

Both in pastoral ministry and in evangelism, preachers face some common problems. We need to confront these and deal with them if we are to minister effectively.

(a) *Our tendency to emulate our heroes.* Certain people are models or mentors to us. We honor them because they've helped us. We are impressed with their gifts and abilities. But a problem arises when I feel I must emulate another person in order to be effective in evangelism, or in any work God calls me to do.

Over the last twenty-five years, I've worked with a number of outstanding people, individuals with marvelous gifts, noteworthy achievements, and the ability to do things I could never do if I spent the rest of my life trying. When I have tried to imitate what they do, I have come off as a failure every time. We need to be set free to use the gifts God has given us.

Leighton Ford has had a great impact throughout the world. But there was a time twenty or so years ago when Billy Graham and Leighton Ford were alternating in preaching on

"The Hour of Decision." Listening to the broadcast, you couldn't tell who was who! Leighton spoke with the same inflection, intonation, and pronunciation, even though he was from Canada and Dr. Graham from North Carolina. Soon Leighton realized, "That's not me"—and part of his greatness is seen in that realization. Leighton Ford's contribution to world Christianity came out of his own gifts, not his imitation of Billy Graham.

(b) *Mixed motives.* In our preaching, especially evangelistic preaching, we need to be as honest and clear as possible about our motivation. It's a heady thing to preach to thousands of people. Dr. Lawrence Lacour used to say, "When we preach, it is either for display or response." I can "preach Christ" with an eye toward displaying my speaking ability. I can "preach Christ," showing people my extensive vocabulary, my clever outline. I can "preach Christ" to impress people because they see I don't use any notes, or that I preach with great erudition. But, when it comes to *motivation*, I'm either there for display, or I'm there for response.

As preachers we are not merely public speakers. We are not on an after-dinner circuit. We are not entertainers. We are called to preach Christ, seeking above all else to introduce those who hear to a compelling Savior in whom they may find life.

Yet if those who hear, who feel the power of God's love, are moved to respond and have no opportunity to do so, we have failed them and they are left frustrated.

People need the opportunity to act. An old cliche says, "Inspiration without expression leads to depression." Even more sobering is the realization that "Inspiration without expression leads to a fatal desensitizing." The call is there, but there is no opportunity to respond. The hearers say, "I want to do something," but they don't know what to do or how to do it. They become increasingly desensitized. The next time the call doesn't mean as much; the next time they flippantly wave it off; the next time it doesn't matter. People, when moved, *need* the opportunity to respond.

(c) *Putting on the pressure.* We live in the kind of culture that puts us in a "no" mode. We are constantly exposed to advertisements, salespeople, telephone solicitations; we are constantly saying no to people, to these pressures.

I learned an important lesson about evangelism some years ago: If you want to put the pressure on, take it off! There's a vast difference between *my* pressure and *God's* pressure. If I want people to feel the pressure of the Holy Spirit, then I must take my pressure off. If, in a Sunday morning service, an evangelistic series, or a revival meeting, people perceive that I'm pressuring them, they will just do what they have been doing all week—say no. They came to the service in a *no* syndrome. Because they were conditioned to say no, the moment they sensed my pressure, it was no again.

Most people are already aware of their guilt. When we lay more on them, we dispense law rather than gospel. The stereotype that preachers judge people with statements like, "You are a sinner," or "You need to repent!" is a half truth. As frequently in the church, the judgment is passed in the other direction. Rather than letting people evaluate and face up to their own spiritual condition, *we tell them* who and what they are. "You are a good Christian." "You are a mainstay in this congregation."

A chairman of a local church board once said to his pastor, "I have not really given my life to Christ. I feel like a hypocrite and have come to you to resign."

"Oh, no, not you, John," the pastor responded. "You are the best Christian in this church!" The man was struggling, trying to look honestly at his own life, and in that moment, rather than listening, hearing, or helping, the pastor passed judgment. We should not assume people have or have not responded to the call of God in Christ.

Part of reducing *our* pressure may also be to send people away from a service graciously with a blessing, even if there has been no response. We must follow the example of Jesus, whose offer of life was freely made. We can never coerce people into loving God.

## Calling for Response

Dr. Donald English from London was a guest preacher in our church a few years ago. People were interested in his visit and came in great numbers to hear him—that particular Sunday we had an "Easter Sunday" attendance! At the end of his sermon, Dr. English did an unexpected thing. It was not an evangelistic series, but he made it that. He said: "We've heard the gospel preached. Some of you here may need to commit yourselves to Christ for the first time. You may want to come forward. But we all need to respond to the gospel in different ways. Today's preaching may be different things for different persons—a deeper commitment, something new we have learned, a challenge to do something, a challenge to give up something, a relationship to be put right. If today the sermon has been any of these things for you, I invite you to come forward, say a prayer at the altar, and then return to your seat. If you wish to stay for counseling and want the minister to talk with you after the service, please do so."

Many people responded. It was a broad invitation, but it was no broader than needs that were represented in that congregation. People needed a chance to respond—not just for the initial act of trusting Christ, but for the problems and sins with which they battle on a daily basis.

For many years Harry Denman was the best-known layman in the Methodist church. Billy Graham once said he was the greatest practitioner of personal evangelism he knew. When I was a college student I heard him preach on Mark 1:15 (KJV): "The time is fulfilled, and the kingdom of God is at hand: repent ye, and believe the gospel." I still vividly recall what he said and did.

After he preached, Dr. Denman walked down to the front of the audience. The people were seated in four sections. He turned to the section on the left and said, "If you feel you can say it, I'd like you to repeat after me: 'I believe that Jesus is Christ, the Son of God.'" Many of the people said it. Then, he went on to the next section. "I believe Jesus is Christ, the Son of God," and on to the next.

He then proposed a second affirmation: "I believe that God raised him from the dead and he is alive." He had each section say it—"I believe that God raised him . . . and he is alive." He gave a third sentence: "I believe that he is able to save any person from the law of sin and death if he will repent and believe—because of my own experience." Each section was given the opportunity to repeat that aloud.

The final affirmation was a promise: "I will tell it with my lips and life." We repeated it section by section. Then he said, "If this is your commitment, write it in the front of your Bible along with the date, and sign your name to it."

I did it! I wrote those affirmations in the Bible which I used for many years: "I believe . . . Because of my experience . . . I will tell it with my lips and life." For me it was a landmark, a milepost. I've read those sentences perhaps a thousand times.

Evangelism is more than enthusiasm, more than passing judgment on the people or manipulating them to respond. If we truly seek to be ourselves and let the Lord, through his Holy Spirit, convict people of sin and draw them to himself, we will see the fruit of our efforts. And those to whom we minister will believe because of their own experience of God's grace and power, and will "tell it with their lips and with their lives."

*Joe Hale is General Secretary of the World Methodist Council. He came to the Council in 1976 following twenty years' service in national and interdenominational evangelism throughout the United States. This chapter is taken from his lecture on "Preparing Evangelistic Messages," given at the Billy Graham School of Evangelism in Asheville, North Carolina, May, 1989.*

# Chapter Eleven
# Linking Up
# With the Source

## *David Tyler Scoates*

Sharing the faith is God's idea. For the Christian, the story of God's reaching out to us is centered in the person of Jesus Christ. The endeavor to bring the Good News of what God has done for us through Jesus Christ is true evangelism.

About three Sundays after I came to Hennepin Avenue United Methodist in Minneapolis, a choir member was overheard asking a friend, "I wonder if he is going to preach about Jesus again today." Our call as ministers of the gospel is to "preach about Jesus again today," to call people to the challenge of following him.

## Fundamental Convictions

(a) *We cannot separate what we say from the people we are.* Our preaching takes place in the context of a pastoral setting; preaching is a pastoral activity. That's where God has placed us, and that's the context in which our preaching must take place. The minister works within an unusual network of trust and intimacy that makes the separation of character from performance impossible. Who we are thunders so loudly that people can't hear what we say.

In other words, the question arises, "Who is preaching?" The whole person, something within, comes out in our words. Not all our laypersons, the church members, expect that. Many of them are under the assumption that "preachers are paid to be good; laypersons are simply good for nothing." Yet our preaching is not born in a vacuum; it comes out of who we are as a person.

(b) *Sermons are not speeches for all occasions.* They are, rather, addresses prepared for one group, at one particular time and place, and generally they are delivered in the context of worship. Worship helps us see the truth; worship points our souls and minds toward God. The sermon is part of a continuing dialogue between the soul and God—a dialogue begun in the hymns, sustained in the prayers, and continued by the sermon.

During the sixteenth-century Reformation, when those reformers made such drastic changes in the Roman Catholic order of worship, the central place which had been taken by the Eucharist was taken over by the sermon. In fact, at the highest point in the Roman Catholic mass, when the priest lifts up the host and rings the bell—at that point the reformers inserted the sermon. The sermon was the climax in worship, the medium through which God spoke or called the people to repentance and Christian discipleship.

That's why preaching is primary in evangelism. Music is important; fellowship is important—but basic to all of it is preaching. And that is a tremendous responsibility to place upon one person standing in a little box Sunday after Sunday.

A minister was rummaging around in an old church attic up in New England a few years ago. He found some old minutes from the Board of Elders meeting. In the minutes, he found a reference that said, "the committee was appointed to investigate the squeak in the pulpit!" There are many times when we feel like only "a squeak in the pulpit." But we need to keep at it with the knowledge that at least someone in the community is attempting to call people to Christian discipleship.

Because it is so important, the sermon should give the

listener something to think about. There is no reason to ask the congregation to park their brains at the front door of the church. We must give them something to think about, something to feel, something to decide, something to do. Ultimately, we must give the listener the generous, genuine invitation to say yes to the claims of Christ.

Our primary task in preaching is to lead people to think about their relationship to Christ, to feel something about their relationship to Christ, to decide on their relationship to Christ. And then we issue the call for them to make a decision for Christ. Every sermon should end with a call for people to live their baptism. When the benediction is given, the service is not over. It is just beginning. We gather to scatter. We preach Christ for a result—so that people will do something with their faith.

Abraham Lincoln often attended the New York Avenue Presbyterian Church in Washington, D.C. He chose the Wednesday evening services so as not to disrupt the Sunday morning worship. The pastor always left his study door open when he knew the President was coming to the service. Mr. Lincoln would sit in the study office just off to the right of the sanctuary. He would leave the door open a bit and listen to the pastor, Dr. Gurley, preach. One Wednesday evening, walking back to the White House, his aide asked Mr. Lincoln his appraisal of the sermon. The President was thoughtful in his reply: "The content was excellent. He delivered with eloquence. He had put work into his message."

"Then you thought it was a great sermon?" asked the aide.

"No," replied the President.

"But you said the content was excellent, it was delivered with eloquence and it showed much work."

"That's true," Mr. Lincoln said, "But Mr. Gurley forgot the most important ingredient. He forgot to ask us to do something great."

Now for all of us the most important ingredient is to present Christ as Savior. Mr. Lincoln's point, however, is well taken. We should have our sermons come out somewhere. We should have persuaded someone to do something with their life. Even something great! One person put it this way: "It is not out of line to ask of a sermon, 'What ultimate vision is held before us?'"

(c) *The sermon is the word of God*, a significant word of God, the eternal word of God. And this is what we are to preach. Congregations do not need oratory. They need insight. They need to look at their lives through the lens of Scripture and theology, to find a fresh perspective for living. Preaching brings the Scriptures forward as the living voice in the congregation. The Scriptures are the normative life of the church, not to be taken for granted, not to be abused, not to be ignored. The Scriptures keep watch over the life and faith of the church and blow the whistle on self-serving sermons.

We are called upon to ask, *What authorizes my sermon?* If the authorization is by the Scriptures, *In what way?* And, *How do I prepare so as to enter the pulpit with some confidence that my understanding of biblical preaching has been implemented with honesty and integrity?* Grappling with the Scriptures is never easy, but being true to the Word of God is of primary importance.

(d) *We must depend on the Holy Spirit in preaching.* The power that transforms a supper into sacrament can transform our words into the word of God.

A preacher was trying to bargain with an automobile dealer over the price of a new car. The minister pleaded with the car salesman by saying, "After all, I'm just a poor preacher." To which the salesman responded, "Yes, I know, I've heard you preach."

We cannot do it alone, nor are we expected to do so. We do not do the converting; the Holy Spirit does. We are to be like John the Baptist, preparing the way for the coming of the Holy Spirit to make a difference in peoples lives. And when we forget that, that's when our ministry is in trouble. We are to be a glove into which the hand of God can fit. And if there was ever a day that called for biblical, Spirit-filled Christians, it is today. This is not the *Titanic* where a lucky few can climb into lifeboats and be rescued. This is *Air Force One*, where there are no parachutes; everyone—president and vice president, Congress, and every citizen, and particularly every preacher of the gos-

pel—must work to present the gospel as clearly and persua-
sively as possible to rescue a morally and spiritually depleted
universe. And we can only do that by the power of God.

## Acting Upon the Word

Beyond zeal, enthusiasm, and decisive preaching, people
have a need for a formal act of commitment. If the proclamation
is worth hearing, then it is worth acting upon. This is why Dr.
Graham ends every crusade with an invitation. The proclamation has been made. The word has been lifted up about what
God has done for us through Jesus Christ. Then the inspiration
of the moment is formalized through the invitation. Ideas that
fail to incite action tend to remain nebulous, and dissipate.
People need to be invited to make a commitment.

Yet, of all the issues involved in faith-sharing, inviting
persons to receive Christ is most often feared, abused, and
misunderstood. Thus I have found in many denominations,
many pastors back away from this crucial aspect of witnessing
to the faith.

## Inviting Failure

Part of the problem in extending the invitation lies in our
failure to stop and define it. "An invitation is a logical, sequential opportunity to accept or reject, or hold in abeyance, one's
proclamation of the Good News. The invitation does not
presuppose a specific response,"[1] but confronts the listener, the
person in the congregation, with the necessity of dealing with
whether they will respond to the proclamation or not.

My friend, the late O. Dean Martin, was a great preacher
and evangelist. We went through seminary together. We lived
in several of the same cities, serving as pastors of different

---

[1]O. Dean Martin, *Invite: Preaching for Response* (Nashville: United Methodist
Publishing House, 1987), 26.

churches. We jogged together. We prayed together. We talked together. We shared together.

About a year before Dean died of a brain tumor, I had long conversations and correspondence with him concerning the whole matter of issuing the invitation, wondering how I could strengthen my ministry through the invitation. Dean shared with me the following ideas.

Often there are roadblocks that prevent an inquirer from making a commitment to Christ, that is, responding to the invitation. "If I preached this Sunday on 'God's Good News for the Cancer of Racial Injustice,'" Dean said, "an appropriate invitation at the end of the proclamation would be to encourage people to look hard at the subject, right now, right in that moment. But, if I preach on race relations and extend the usual 'invitation to Christian discipleship,' people in the congregation who have a racial bias, probably already members of the church, wonder why in the world the crazy minister is giving an invitation to Christian discipleship. They are already Christian disciples; and thus they are eased out of any kind of commitment to the whole subject of racial injustice. The conclusion of the service must be invitational, and the invitation must be logical and sequential.

"For example, in the sermon on racial injustice, the worship hour might be concluded by asking the congregation to bow their heads and make their pew an altar of prayer. Then I could say, 'Maybe you're here this morning, and you have never surrendered your inadequacies to God, and thus you are dependent on hostilities toward other races. Will you surrender all of this in prayer right now as you sit there in silence?'

"We are not dictating a specific response, mandating an acceptable reaction. We are extending a sequential invitation, presenting a logical opportunity for racial justice. Or, if we preach on missions, we should extend an invitation that will enable our listeners to respond to a new awakening concerning missions. If we preach on stewardship, the invitation should flow logically from the flow of the sermon—an invitation to make a commitment concerning stewardship. If we speak on family relations, then it should flow toward family relations and a commitment along those lines. If prayer, then prayer; or if Christian service, then Christian service. We need to submit a soft confrontational experience that is sequential.

"Another failure is the failure to extend any invitation at all. Invitations are expected in our culture. People do not want to be pressured, but they know something is wrong if they are not given the opportunity, the chance, to make a decision. If I sell cars and believe in my product, I'm expected eventually to say to a person, 'Will you buy?' When we endeavor to persuade through our preaching without granting an honest opportunity to respond, not only do we fail, but we become poor stewards of God's grace.

"Evangelism is studying, praying, and working hard to bring the Good News of what God has done for us through Jesus Christ. And the committed, caring, prepared preacher says, 'Here is what I believe to be God's Good News for our need. Will you say yes, no, or maybe? What are you going to say?' We must give them the opportunity to respond to the Good News."

## Five Questions

Dean said there are five important questions we need to ask ourselves as we prepare for preaching. Once we've asked ourselves, *What do we mean by invitation?* and have determined to extend the invitation, then as we prepare to proclaim the Word with the invitation in mind, we ought to think about these five questions:

(1) *Do I want anything to happen in this experience of worship?* A lot of times we don't want anything to happen. We're not sure we could handle it if something did happen, if the Holy Spirit did break out in our churches. In the sixteenth century, after the fire that devastated much of London, the city officials decided that they wanted to rebuild London and make it a new London, to build new foundations and new buildings, with some sort of pattern and system to it. So they hired Sir

Christopher Wren, the noted British architect, to develop a plan for the new London. He did so, but there was so much bickering over the new plan, so much delay over it, that people soon despaired, and began to rebuild their homes and their shops on the old foundations. The new London never happened. People went back to their old foundations and rebuilt. That's often what happens in a church. We simply build on the old foundations. We don't really want anything new to happen.

I have on my desk a two-word question, a constant reminder to me as I am preparing my sermon. The question is: *So what?* Am I preparing a sermon simply to tickle the intellectual interest of certain members of the congregation, to please a segment of my congregation, or to please myself? What difference is the message going to make? Is it going to lead toward decision-making? I may be fearful about the invitation, but I'm willing to be vulnerable, run some risk, feel uncomfortable and unsure, because that is my task. I enter the service as the proclaimer, and I want to enter it expectantly. I want God to move, to speak, to heal, to persuade. I want lives to be different when they exit. Little or nothing will happen unless there is within us an expectant faith.

(2) *What do I want to happen?* If I go into a service wanting to see results at the end of that service, often I'm frustrated. "We are commissioned simply to break up fallow ground. We go in and turn over the soil, someone comes along behind us and plants the seed in the ground now turned over and prepared for planting. Someone else may come behind and do the watering and the cultivating. Then the bright and wonderful day comes when someone else may actually reap the harvest of this Spirit-led effort."[2]

When we raise the question, *What do I want to see happen?* the answer usually is, *I want to see the harvest.* That, however, may not be God's assignment for us. It may be that we are simply a part of the process, getting ready for God's Spirit to move in that church and to move in the lives of certain people, and those decisions will not come until later.

---

[2]Ibid, 49.

(3) *Is there a logical sequence?* "Decisive, invitational ministry must be predicated on a logical connection between the purpose of the sermon and the response sought."[3]

(4) *Is there clarity of explanation?* "If the closing of the worship service is to be the least bit different, before I begin the sermon I explain thoroughly to the congregation how I want them to consider ending their worship experience. I can usually illustrate the closing experience in the rationale of the sermon. Then when I finish the sermon, I once again thoroughly explain the closing of the service."[4] Certain congregations need time to absorb what's going to happen in the experience of worship as it comes down to a close.

(5) *Am I being sensitive to personal response thresholds?* Am I aware of the personal response thresholds of the people in my congregation? "Not only must people be left to say yes or no or maybe; they must also be left to themselves to begin where they are, and to respond as they can to the claim of God on their lives. In short, everyone has a personal response threshold."[5] Some people respond very quickly to a sequential and intelligible invitation, others must struggle with it and work through their response. And they might even do it in some other way. For example, rather than responding to your invitation at the conclusion of the service, they may come to the office, or invite the pastor to their home to talk about it.

In my particular denomination, people need the space to respond in their own way. The church is full of "ecclesiastical cobblers"—those who have certain expectations that when people come to Christ, they must come a certain way, in a certain worship service, and they must come in response to a certain invitation. Then they must use certain language, and in some cases, even dress a certain way. I call them ecclesiastical cobblers because often, when these people come into the church, they try to put the same shoe on everyone. Then people go hobbling around in the faith, and we say, "Why aren't you

---

[3]Ibid, 51.
[4]Ibid, 52.
[5]Ibid.

leaping for joy? You're a Christian now. Why are you hobbling?"

And they respond, "It's because of this blamed shoe. It doesn't fit." Everyone has a different response threshold, and we cannot expect everyone to come to the Lord the same way.

## Inquirers' Roadblocks

Often a person is struggling with misconceptions or even fears about God or Christ that go clear back to childhood. In other words, a person may feel God's call in her life, and she wants to respond because of something else going on in her life, she has trouble responding. If the preacher talks about God as loving father and she had an abusive father, then that could well be a roadblock for her in coming into a relationship with Christ. Every person is an individual, and brings a particular history to that moment when we issue the invitation. Many of them bring ghosts and a lot of garbage from the past. God can get that out of their system, but they may need help in the process.

Another roadblock is the preconceived idea of *how* people ought to come to God through Christ. They may have heard their entire life that they are supposed to respond in a particular way or with particular words or with a particular attitude, and it simply does not fit them. We should let God do with each person what God will do with him or her. Let God speak to them and move them in a way that fits them. And we are simply to enable them in the process of moving into a whole new relationship with God through Jesus Christ.

## Help for Those Who Counsel

We are simply to be channels of God's love, God's grace. As we counsel someone inquiring about the faith, we need to be sensitive to where that person is. Like the ecclesiastical cobbler we want people to come to where we are. But people are at different points in their spiritual growth, in their spiritual journey, and we must start with them where they are. We are to be channels of God's grace. We are to be vehicles of God to help slowly move that person along to a deeper and more abiding relationship with God.

## After the Invitation

After a person has responded to the invitation, what do we do? One approach is to ask inquirers why they came and what they want God to do in their lives. Then we give them time to pray in their own words. A second approach might be to help them word a prayer; some people don't feel right about praying. They feel they don't know the right words to talk to God.

We, of course, will want to share Scripture with them and give then some practical suggestions that will guide them over the coming days. A simple, brief encounter at the altar after the benediction is not a worthy response to the occasion. It requires tuning in to who that person is, where they are, and helping respond to their particular situation with concrete suggestions and spiritual support that will enable them to grow in their faith.

I have noticed at Dr. Graham's crusades, when the sermon is over and the invitation has been extended and thousands come from all over the stadium or auditorium down to the front and the television cameras are turned off, that Dr. Graham spends a great deal of time talking with those who have responded to his invitation. He will talk to them about the emotional ups and downs of their new commitment. It is going to make a change in their lives, in the lives of those around them, and that for many of them it will not be easy. In other words, Dr. Graham prepares them for those dark moments, the moment of doubt and temptation, the low moments. He then encourages them to become involved in a church, in private prayer, in prayer groups, in Bible studies, and in corporate worship.

The invitation does not conclude when the person comes

forward and responds with a public confession of faith. It continues with our follow-up with the infant Christian.

## Models for Invitation

There is no one model that fits every pastor or every situation.

Often at the close of the service the pastor will ask the congregation to bow their heads and consider carefully and prayerfully the key idea of the sermon and to respond from their place in the pew with their own commitment.

A variation of this approach is, of course, to invite people to come down to the altar for private prayer and perhaps prayer with the pastor and congregation prior to the benediction.

Sometimes a preacher will invite the congregation to give a written response. Many pastors keep three-by-five blank cards in the envelope racks in the pews. Thus they are available for people to write down their response or prayer requests or concerns. One pastor had all the cards collected by the ushers and brought them forward and placed them on the communion table or the altar for a prayer by the pastor.

Some pastors use Holy Communion, the Lord's Supper, as an opportunity to encourage people to give evidence of their decision. If a person gives an indication that they are responding to the invitation, the pastor might kneel with them in prayer after they have received Communion.

Lawrence of Arabia, that colorful character from British history, led the Arabs in their fight against the Turks. Lawrence once brought a group of his Arab friends to London to show them the sights. But what fascinated them the most was the bathroom in their hotel! When Lawrence checked out of the hotel, he couldn't find his Arab friends anywhere. He finally found them gathered in one of the bathrooms. They had found a wrench, and they were trying to take the faucet off the wall. "Lawrence," they said, "this is the gift of Allah. We take this back to our tents in the desert, and we shall never be without water again."

He had to explain to them that that faucet was connected to a pipe behind the wall. They couldn't see it, but nevertheless, it was there. "And that pipe goes down through the hotel and connects with a larger pipe. And that pipe," he said, "goes under the street and connects with a still larger pipe. And that pipe makes its way through the great city of London, and at last connects up with a giant reservoir of water. And," he concluded, "unless that faucet is connected up to the source of water, it's useless."

Unless our ministries are connected to the source of Living Water, we will experience futility and frustration and anxiety and burnout. Only when we are linked up to the source can God begin to move in a church and change lives, including our own lives. We then cannot help but extend the invitation in a variety of ways, to a variety of souls, who have a variety of needs at any particular moment. And God's Spirit will move them to make that decision as a result of the proclamation of God's Good News.

*David Tyler Scoates has pastored several churches in Florida, has served as Vice President of Garrett-Evangelical Theological Seminary, and since 1984 has been Senior Minister of Hennepin Avenue United Methodist Church in Minneapolis. He has served on the boards of numerous organizations, and initiated several interracial social work programs. This chapter is taken from two of his recent addresses, "The Primacy of Preaching," and "Giving an Invitation for Commitment," given at the Billy Graham School of Evangelism, Wheaton, Illinois, June 1987.*

# Chapter Twelve
# The Appeal
# for Decision

*Billy Graham*

A man once got a job sorting potatoes—culling the small ones
out and packing the larger. But the problem was, there were too
many middle-sized potatoes. After three weeks he said to his
boss, "I quit!"

"Why?" asked the boss. "We pay you well."

"I know," replied the man. "It's those infernal decisions!"

Decisions, large and small, are part of our daily lives. A
personal decision precedes any valid commitment. At the
marriage altar the minister asks, "Do you take this woman . . . ?"
And the man responds, "I do." The minister makes the appeal,
and the positive response works an incredible change in two
lives.

In court, the bailiff asks the plaintiff and defendant, "Do
you swear to tell the truth, the whole truth, and nothing but the
truth, so help you God?" The "I do" response validates the
legality of the proceedings.

In a democratic government, our vote at the ballot box
decides which candidate will serve. We are given a choice, and
a decision must be made.

We are, in fact, faced with decisions every hour of the day.
What will I wear? What will I eat for breakfast? How will I get

to work? What is my plan for the day? Most are not life-and-death decisions, but personal decision is required.

A person who senses the spiritual emptiness of life is like the man pursued by his enemies, who comes to a raging river. He must decide if he will stay where he is and face certain death, or cross over and be safe. His life from that moment on will be determined by the choice he makes. But when the man chooses to cross over to safety, he discovers the river is too swift and wide to cross, and there is no bridge. How can he cross over and be safe?

Our great privilege as evangelists is to call on men and women to cross the river and find life—and to tell them the Good News of the bridge God has built for them in the person of his Son Jesus Christ.

Some churchmen ask, "Is it valid or legitimate to extend an invitation for people to come to Christ?" The biblical answer is, "Yes!" Jesus himself said to his disciples, "Follow me"—a call for a personal and verifiable decision.

The evangelistic invitation is valid first because the gospel demands decision; and second, because it is illustrated repeatedly in the Bible.

The gospel of Jesus Christ demands decision. It is not merely a set of facts to which a person can give intellectual agreement; it is a call for an individual to turn in repentance from his sin and his neglect of God—to turn to Christ in faith, accepting him as Lord and Savior. As this happens, a person experiences conversion.

The works of many theologians on conversion, as well as the Bible itself, reveal conversion as a profound mystery. Theologians have debated for centuries about the relationship between the sovereignty of God and human responsibility. It seems to me, however, that both are taught in Scripture and both are involved in conversion. The Bible stresses that in conversion God is at work *and* people must respond.

*God is at work in conversion.* We must always remember that the Holy Spirit is the great Communicator and the great Follow-up Agent. Without the supernatural work of the Spirit there would be no conversion. The Holy Spirit brings conviction of sin; he applies the truth of the gospel. Jesus said, "When he comes, he will convict the world of guilt in regard to sin and righteousness and judgment" (John 16:8). First Thessalonians 1:5 (KJV) says, "For our gospel came not unto you in word only, but also in power, and in the Holy Ghost." The Holy Spirit brings new birth and new life. Jesus told Nicodemus that unless people are born again they "cannot enter the kingdom of God" (John 3:5). The Bible says that "he saved us, not because of righteous things we had done, but because of his mercy. He saved us through the washing of rebirth and renewal by the Holy Spirit" (Titus 3:5). This great truth should make us more and more dependent on God in our evangelism, knowing that ultimately it is God who changes lives; we are helpless apart from him.

*People must respond.* But we also need to remember that the Bible underlines the necessity of human response to the gospel. Jesus said, "No man, having put his hand to the plough, and looking back, is fit for the kingdom of God" (Luke 9:62, KJV). We must not imply that following Christ is easy. It is tough and challenging. Jesus let people know the cost of following him. "Strait is the gate, and narrow is the way, which leadeth unto life, and few there be that find it" (Matthew 7:14, KJV). "If any man will come after me, let him deny himself, and take up his cross, and follow me" (Matthew 16:24, KJV).

When the Arctic explorer Sir Ernest Henry Shackleton ran an ad in a New York paper to recruit men for his venture, the ad read: "Wanted: Men to spend several months in the Arctic—long hours, low pay, meager food, and poor accommodations." That ad broke all the newspaper records in response to a "help-wanted" ad!

Conversion is more than a psychological phenomenon—it is the turning of the whole person to God. It is a conscious commitment to Christ, involving repentance and faith. In the gospel, men and women are called to make Christ Lord of every aspect of life. He is to be our life's priority! We are to follow Jesus Christ in discipleship.

Such discipleship is not only an *emotional* appeal to feel sorry for sins and to turn to righteousness. It is not only an *intellectual* appeal to accept the teaching of Jesus and imitate his example. It is not only a *religious* appeal to submit to certain ritual acts. The invitation is essentially a *personal* appeal of unqualified self-commitment to the person of Jesus Christ.

From "Adam, where art thou?" in Genesis 3, to the final appeal of the Spirit and the bride in Revelation 22, the Bible is one re-echoing invitation to lost humanity to turn to God.

Moses issued an invitation when he said, "Whoever is for the Lord, come to me" (Exodus 32:26).

Joshua appealed to Israel to make a definite commitment: "Choose for yourselves this day whom you will serve" (Joshua 24:15). When the people said they would decide for God and serve him, Joshua wrote it down and had a great stone set up as a witness to their decision.

Elijah confronted the false prophets of Baal and the unbelief of the people on Mount Carmel. "Elijah said to all the people, 'Come here to me.' They came to him, and he repaired the altar of the Lord, which was in ruins" (1 Kings 18:30). When God miraculously consumed the sacrifice on the altar, the people responded, "The Lord—he is God! The Lord—he is God!" (1 Kings 18:39).

John the Baptist preached in the wilderness, and multitudes came to hear him and respond to his call for repentance (Mark 1:5).

Jesus said to Peter and Andrew, "Come, follow me, . . . and I will make you fishers of men" (Matthew 4:19).

With the possible exception of Nicodemus, everyone Jesus ever called was either called to declare publicly for him, or else Jesus spoke to them in front of others. A public decision confirms the personal commitment of the heart.

Not every person who comes to Christ will come in some public forum, of course. The greatest Christian I know is my wife, and she cannot remember the day or the hour when she received Christ. But at some point, she made her commitment public. When Jesus was walking from Jericho to Jerusalem, a blind man named Bartimaeus cried out to him. "Jesus stood and commanded him to be brought unto him" (Luke 18:40, KJV). Jesus could have quietly gone to the man on the sidelines, but instead he called him forward publicly. In front of a vast throng of people, Jesus looked up in a tree and called Zacchaeus to come down publicly (Luke 19:5).

Jesus instructed his disciples that, when they preached the gospel, they were to make it clear that men must respond. "Whoever acknowledges me before men, I will also acknowledge him before my Father in heaven. But whoever disowns me before men, I will disown him before my Father in heaven" (Matthew 10:32–33).

The apostles followed Christ's pattern. On the day of Pentecost, Peter urged people to repent and believe in Jesus, and three thousand came to Christ—somebody counted them! When Paul looked back over his ministry in Ephesus, he could say, "For three years I never stopped warning each of you night and day with tears" (Acts 20:31). As a result, a strong church was established as people responded in repentance and faith. In 2 Corinthians 5:20, Paul declares, "We are therefore Christ's ambassadors, as though God were making his appeal through us. We implore you on Christ's behalf: Be reconciled to God." The gospel always demands decision. That is why the appeal for decision is so important in the work of evangelism.

The call for decision—the invitation—is therefore not something just added to the end of an evangelistic sermon as an afterthought. Instead, the whole sermon leads toward it. Whether it is a public decision then and there, or a private decision in the quietness of one's home, it is not only valid to issue an invitation, it is essential. The invitation may take many forms, but if people hear our message and go away without having been confronted with the clear-cut call, "What do you think about the Christ?" (Matthew 22:42), then we have failed in our proclamation of the gospel. We need to make that call to decision clearly, effectively, and boldly.

## Preparation for the Invitation

The most important preparation an evangelist can make for the invitation is personal, spiritual preparation. This is true for everything we do as evangelists, of course; for if our hearts are not right before God and our lives are not pure, then we cannot expect him to bless our ministry. This is especially true of the invitation.

Every time I give an invitation, I am in an attitude of prayer inwardly, because I know I am totally dependent on God. This is the moment that I feel emotionally, physically, and spiritually drained. This is the part of the evangelistic service that often exhausts me physically. A great spiritual battle is going on in the hearts of many people. With me, it becomes a spiritual battle of such proportions that sometimes I feel almost faint. There is an inward groaning and agonizing in prayer that I cannot possibly put into words.

Our sermons should be bathed in prayer, our meetings should be undergirded with prayer. Time after time in my own ministry, I have seen God work in unusual ways, and found out only later that God's people in that area had been praying earnestly—sometimes for years. Some planted the seed, others watered it, "but God made it grow" (1 Corinthians 3:6).

## The Purpose of Invitation

The invitation is not simply a neat wrap-up of a preaching service. It is the focus, the crucial climax of speaking the Word to others. The invitation has profound and far-reaching consequences for the hearer.

*An invitation makes it clear to our listeners that the gospel demands decision.* People cannot remain neutral about Christ. Not to decide is to decide not to.

*We invite people at that moment to indicate an affirmative response to Christ's call to commitment.* In some places where evangelism must be done quietly, it could be a handshake, or a nodding of a head. In other situations, it could be the signing of a card, the raising of a hand, or better yet (if the situation allows it), asking them to come forward to the front of the auditorium or to a side room for a brief after-meeting of instruction. I have used all these methods of invitation.

I have preached in some places where all I could do is to ask people to bow their heads for a few moments of silence and make the commitment in their hearts. But in my own experience, this has been the exception rather than the norm.

*By giving an invitation, we identify and help conserve the results of the preaching of the gospel.* That is why in our crusades, whenever possible, a counselor obtains the name and address of the person who has come forward; then there can be follow-up so that an inquirer will be put in touch with other believers. A number of years ago we decided to call the people who come forward and respond to an invitation "inquirers" rather than "decisions" or "converts," because only God the Holy Spirit really knows what is happening in their hearts.

*An invitation can be a means of assurance to a person.* In later years, that person can look back to a decisive moment when he or she made a public decision for Christ. Some years ago, the great German theologian Helmut Thielicke attended one of our crusades. He wrote me the most magnificent letter on how the invitation had affected him, and how I should never preach without giving one. The memory of that moment reminds people of their vow to follow Christ, and of Christ's promise of forgiveness.

*People may respond to the call for decision for various reasons.* We often direct our evangelistic sermons at people who have never come to Christ, and give an invitation for them to accept him as their Lord and Savior. And yet it has been my experience that many people respond for various *other* reasons. Some believers who have wandered from the Lord may want to recommit their lives to him. Others may not be sure that they are saved and are seeking assurance. Still others desperately want to talk with someone about a problem they have.

Although most of my own experience is with the mass meeting, I have also had the privilege of conducting evangelistic services in small churches, and in "brush arbor" meetings, where people from a village gathered around. In such a case (as I have already pointed out), the method of invitation would vary from a highly organized and controlled meeting such as an auditorium or a stadium. I did a great deal of my early preaching on street corners, where I asked people to lift their hands, and after the closing prayer to see me personally.

In the one-to-one evangelistic encounters, asking for a decision from just one person is often difficult. But it is extremely important that we have the boldness and courage to do so—if we are led by the Holy Spirit, and if the circumstances permit. I believe it is biblical and appropriate to ask people to give an outward sign of the inward contract they have made with the Lord Jesus Christ, just as a salesman asks a person to "sign on the dotted line" or agree with a handshake when he is selling a product.

## The Focus of the Message

The entire evangelistic sermon should be directed toward the invitation. Everything in the sermon should, directly or indirectly, point toward the call for decision we will make. An evangelistic sermon makes people see who they are in the light of God's Word. It makes them see what they must do in response. That is one reason I have often found it helpful to confront people with the call to decision throughout the sermon.

I don't call them forward several times, of course, but I ask questions throughout the sermon—and not just at the end, such as, "Have you ever really trusted Christ?" or, "Do you know that if you died right now you would go to heaven?" I give statements that make it clear that the gospel demands decision, such as, "You can't remain neutral about Christ," or, "Let Christ come into your life right now and cleanse you from your sins and give you a new purpose for living." Throughout the sermon, therefore, I often try to make it clear that the gospel demands decision involving the intellect and the emotions, but primarily the will. The whole sermon should reinforce that fact and point toward the invitation.

In some sermons we may want to deal with the barriers some people have to overcome before they will respond. Some are barriers that unbelievers have in their minds—often not intellectual problems so much as problems with the will, peer pressure, false views of God, or a reluctance to turn from sin. Sometimes people don't respond simply because they don't believe they need to do so—because they have been baptized, for example, or are members of a church. Such misunderstanding happens especially in parts of America and western Europe.

We often think of western Europe and America as the fountainhead of Christianity. Christ, however, was born, lived, taught, and died in that part of the world that touches Asia, Africa, and Europe. In historical terms, Christianity is an Eastern faith, and often adapts itself more easily to Eastern thinking and lifestyle. In western Europe, church attendance is so low and the influence of the church so weak that it startles Christians from such places as East Africa, Northeast India, Latin America, or even those from North America. Western Europe has become one of the great mission fields of the world, and often the hindrances to faith come in the form of a deep-seated religious heritage that substitutes for a living relationship with Jesus Christ.

We must speak to the needs of those who hear us. We need to understand the barriers that some of them face and speak to them directly so that they will be open to the invitation to receive Christ.

## Method of Invitation

While there will always be special aspects or elements because of cultural differences and the way we preach, certain guidelines about the call to decision are very important. At least two, I believe, are essential.

First, we need to clarify what we are asking people to *believe*.

We are inviting people to commit their lives to Christ as his disciples. And the cost is high. I've seen some invitations lower the cost of discipleship. Thus in my own crusades, I do not invite people forward to join an organization or a church, nor do I invite them for baptism, or any other reason except to receive Christ. It is our privilege as evangelists to invite people to make the most important decision they will ever make—one which has eternal consequences. We need to make the choice as clear as possible and concentrate on that decision.

Second, we must make it clear what people are to actually *do*—and repeat it several times: coming forward, lifting a hand, going to a separate room (or whatever method is being used), or going home and making a commitment.

A clearly defined act of commitment will not only avoid confusion, but it may remove a barrier in some minds. Many people will not take any action if they feel they are facing an unknown situation. The mechanics of an invitation should never be a barrier to people coming to Christ.

An invitation usually will consist of at least three elements. First, there will be an appeal for people to accept Christ by repentance and faith. Second, there will be a brief explanation of how we are asking people to respond. A third element— perhaps not, strictly speaking, part of the invitation, although it should be closely related to it—is the follow-up message we may speak to those who have responded. Often, the follow-up instruction is actually an invitation, because in it we outline the gospel clearly and simply, perhaps lead them in a prayer of commitment, and explain what has happened to them and how they can grow spiritually.

If possible, those who respond should talk individually with someone who can help them. It may be the evangelist, a pastor, or trained counselors, but inquirers need that personal touch. For many years we have had a program of training counselors before a crusade. Many people have told us it was the most important result of the crusade, because a large number of soul-winners had been trained to bring people to Christ—not only during the crusade, but for years to come.

It is a great privilege to be used of God to point people to Jesus Christ and invite men and women to commit their lives to him. Part of the gift of an evangelist is the gift of giving the invitation with directness and yet sensitivity. But like any other gift which God may give us, it must be sharpened and used for his glory.

*This chapter is taken from Dr. Graham's message, "The Evangelist's Appeal for Decision," delivered at the 1986 International Conference for Itinerant Evangelists in Amsterdam.*